TROPICS OF TEACHING:
PRODUCTIVITY, WARFARE, AND PRIESTHOOD

Teacher education and research on teaching are surrounded by 'a culture of niceness' that can prevent the expression of problems experienced by teachers and researchers. Based on the premise that deconstruction and demystification are a necessary counterforce to 'shared myths,' *Tropics of Teaching* offers a provocative, original assessment of mass educational concepts and teacher education, leading to the challenge of rethinking pedagogy in general.

François Tochon identifies three shaping metaphors – 'productivity' (output standardization; business efficiency), 'warfare' (strategy; expertise), and 'priesthood' (the enlightened subject) – which he argues stifle individual growth in a classroom context. He then advocates an entirely different approach, which he terms 'a countermethodology of self-reflection, rather than an incursion into the life of the Other.' This approach is achieved, in part, via a technique he calls action poetry: a means of research and educational activism.

Tochon's original contribution to educational scholarship – and his direct challenge to educators themselves – is the practice of reflective, situated research with classroom observation (his own journal entries are included in the text). *Tropics of Teaching* is a call to education specialists and to scholars in social literary studies to rethink current education curricula, policies, and philosophies.

(Toronto Studies in Semiotics and Communication)

FRANÇOIS TOCHON is a professor at the University of Wisconsin-Madison in the Department of Curriculum and Instruction. He has written eighteen books and more than one hundred articles and book chapters.

FRANÇOIS TOCHON

Tropics of Teaching: Productivity, Warfare, and Priesthood

UNIVERSITY OF TORONTO PRESS
Toronto Buffalo London

© University of Toronto Press Incorporated 2002
Toronto Buffalo London
Printed in Canada

ISBN 0-8020-3685-6 (cloth)

Printed on acid-free paper

Toronto Studies in Semiotics and Communication
Editors: Marcel Danesi, Umberto Eco, Paul Perron, Peter Schulz,
Thomas A. Sebeok

National Library of Canada Cataloguing in Publication

Tochon, François Victor, 1954–
    Tropics of teaching : productivity, warfare, and priesthood /
François Tochon.

    (Toronto studies in semiotics and communication)
    Includes bibliographical references and index.
    ISBN 0-8020-3685-6

    1. Teachers – Training of.   2. Teaching.   I. Title.   II. Series.

    LB1051.T587 2002   370′.71   C2002-902695-4

University of Toronto Press acknowledges the financial assistance
to its publishing program of the Canada Council for the Arts and the
Ontario Arts Council.

This book has been published with the help of a grant from the Humanities
and Social Sciences Federation of Canada, using funds provided by the
Social Sciences and Humanities Research Council of Canada.

University of Toronto Press acknowledges the financial support for
its publishing activities of the Government of Canada through the
Book Publishing Industry Development Program (BPIDP).

Contents

Acknowledgments

The preparation of this book was supported by a research grant. I am grateful to the Social Sciences and Humanities Research Council of Canada (SSHRC) for enabling me to contribute to the study of reflectivity in teacher education. Moreover, the SSHRC awarded a publication grant for this book. Positions taken in the book are not necessarily those of the Council. I thank Virginia Richardson for her reading of an early version of chapter 1, and Jamie-Lynn Magnusson for her discussion of the second chapter. I thank Sue, a Manitoba middle-school teacher, for letting her diary pierce deconstruction. Sue expresses her identity in claiming a scholarly voiceful anonymity – she does not want to be networked. Also, I thank Rina Kampeas for her help in translation or linguistic revision of the essays on which this book was based, and most of all for her friendship.

I wish to acknowledge the publishers who authorized the publication here of work previously presented in their journals: *Curriculum Studies* and *Pedagogy, Culture and Society* (Triangle, U.K.) for chapters 1 and 2, the *International Journal of Applied Semiotics* for chapter 3, *Atwood* for chapter 4, *Art and Learning Research* for chapter 5, and the *Journal of Curriculum Studies* (U.S.) for the afterword. Also I have to thank Éditions 'Prise de Parole' (Sudbury, Ontario) for authorizing republication of Jean-Marc Dalpé's poems in chapter 5.

Finally, I am deeply grateful to my wife, Isabelle, whose belief in me remained unwavering, for forbearance during a long spell of obsessive work. This dedication says only a fraction of what it means.

TROPICS OF TEACHING:
PRODUCTIVITY, WARFARE, AND PRIESTHOOD

Introduction

This book could be characterized as a series of essays demystifying crucial issues in teacher education and research on teaching. The demystification process starts with denouncing shared myths and deconstructing their expression, because such myths can relate to diverse intentions. The same idea, the same word of wisdom, can be used to enhance or to demolish. Behind educational beliefs stands the intention to uplift or to degrade. Words may hide implicit targets and prevent the free development of the potential for thought and action. Deregulation, standardization, professionalization: such key ideas hide highly politicized agendas and ideological battlefields (Cochran-Smith & Fries, 2001). When mass concepts are disseminated in such a way that their language is enforced as the ultimate Good, their deconstruction becomes a necessity. Deconstruction is characterized here as the positive use of criticism to counterbalance the negative effects of constructive modelling that are possible when niceness prevails in dialogue and prevents the expression of real problems. I therefore understand deconstruction to be a complementary and necessary part of any constructive, structural process.

Deconstructive analysis consists of first locating basic binary contradictions in a proposed model and then undoing the structure of these oppositions, which organize established values and power (Hlynka, 1989; Scholes, 1985). Deconstruction is linked to the idea of the impossibility of taking a metacritical position and finding an ultimate meaning. Its processes subvert the unarticulated presuppositions of idealist discourse, which, when they remain implicit, maintain dominance networks within a culture. Deconstruction has had its most sensational results in unravelling the discourse of science – for even science is grounded in rhetorical language. Besides reversing binary oppositions, the process of deconstruction uses displacement, parody, and paraphrastic expositions of extended metaphors.

The word *tropics* comes from the etymological roots *tropos* and *tropikos* in Greek and *tropi* in Latin, which mean 'turns,' 'manners,' and later 'metaphors.' The English *trope* inherits its attributes: it is a matter of style, a deviation from pure logic to access feeling. That is, figures of speech lead to new meanings. In his major work *Tropics of Discourse: Essays in Cultural Criticism* (1978), Hayden White explored the relationship between historical writing and literary forms, and the role of tropes in both forms of writing. His interpretation of history as novel, along the line of Vico, Derrida, and Foucault, shed a new light on the intertwining of figurative language and the creation of truths. Indeed, narrative strategies reshape history and characterize the objects of our representations of the reality. The fictions of the historian face the realities of the novelist. In both cases, narrative is not a recording but a redescription and a recoding of reality into a new mode of thinking. 'Troping is the soul of discourse' (ibid., p. 2). Experience is continuously metaphorized to value certain aspects of reality. Even research findings project onto their data the interpretation that they metaphorically mould. In that sense discourse on reality must create myths to become effective.

The deciphering of metaphors woven through a text, the undoing of structures of concealment, reveals the text's self-transgressions (Spivak in Derrida, 1976). In a mass system, teacher-education models may appear as simplified realities, extended metaphors, and thus 'language games' (Lyotard, 1993; Wittgenstein, 1999). In my approach, however, I diverge intentionally from the already divergent French deconstructionist schools, in that I believe deconstruction is not a ludic end in itself but rather should lead to cautious reconstruction. My deconstruction of deconstruction leads me to an integrated deconstructionism, arguing the romantic aspects of postmodern deconstruction. To use Lather's term (1992), my proposal is 'postparadigmatic'; that is, it may be difficult to attach it to any existing paradigm. I do not pretend to represent an authorized voice, but I hope others will recognize their own challenges in mine.

I will therefore use deconstruction here in its fullest and, probably, its most interesting sense. This approach can be refreshing and challenging, as will be shown in chapter 1. The chapter discusses three castes in teacher education – three trends metaphorically shaped by productivity, warfare, and priesthood. The first is mastery learning and output standardization, that is, the discourse that uses the language of productivity and efficiency. The second trend is strategic teaching, the discourse that targets expertise. The third trend is narrative awakening, the discourse of the enlightened subject. My objective is their deconstruction: mass educational concepts, even positive ones, can stifle individual growth, responsibility, and difference. To this end, I also discuss the future of reflective trends in teacher education.

Chapter 2 discusses the philosophical roots of educational narratology, and schematically lays a methodological groundwork for analysing and understanding the narratives that construct meaning in a pedagogical setting. This chapter explores the philosophical and semiotic implications of educational acts of meaning making that are mediated through narrative inquiry. I discuss the risks of a narrative view of teacher education as it is related to the 'I'-philosophy tradition of subjective idealism. Indeed, modelling the Self may be an invitation to indoctrination. Consequently I offer deconstructive ways of critically analysing stories of narrative educators, which may prevent the mere imposition of influence networks for the sake of personal awakening.

The third chapter addresses a significant educational issue, namely the narrative transformation of lived experience for the purpose of understanding and reflection. I propose a countermethodology of self-reflection rather than an incursion into the life of the other. The chapter launches a dialogue between roles, processes, beliefs, and ways of knowing, within a cross-cultural ethic. This ethic is based on naturalistic data collected while doing reflective, situated research with classroom observations. The object of study is both the classroom teaching context and the situated researcher. At the time of the research, I had migrated from Switzerland to live for ten years in Canada. The flashbacks of my past identities expressed in diaries of school research echo my reflections while moving to the United States. Access to another culture is always a surprise. I wilfully resist the temptation of structure, structure that would misleadingly suggest a definitive truth, and this resistance guides the controlled drift of conceptual connections. It is also a reflection on borders.

While chapter 3 focuses on time and storied reflection in relation to lived observations, chapter 4 turns to the semiotics of educational spaces: What are the signs and meaning of educational space-sharing? I consider a neo-Aristotelian and neo-Avicennian interpretation of spaces of interaction. Individuals may be geographically close yet unable to cooperate, because they are not attuned to the same semiotic territory. Semiotic territories are stratified to establish congruence among those belonging to the same semiotic 'beams.' Families of signs characterize each space of meaning, whose inhabitants are linked conceptually. Symbols and metaphors produce a consensual effect among attuned participants belonging to the same beam of meaning. Epistemic borders are translucent when seen through the light of meaning beams – even the border between art and science is fuzzy. Art and science rest on a set of paradigmatic connections that emerge from communitarian practices based on the establishment of rules and local values. They come from historicized actions and thus from story telling. Education does not escape this establishment of rules and discourse formalism. Educational story telling can also turn into action, what I will name *didaction*.

Before speaking about didaction, it would be good to say something about a new, international trend of curriculum research called *didactics*. Didactics articulates experience as the meeting point of learner's knowledge, teacher's knowledge, and curricular, cultural knowledge. This junction point, experience, is studied within educational encounters and situations. Experience permeates subject-matter planning and instructional design. It is embedded in local cultures for which curricula are but artefacts that allow the exchange of significations and meaning-making processes. European curricula are grounded in this root conception, and shaped within didactics as a field of knowledge.

In Germanic, francophone, and Hispanic countries around the world, curriculum and instruction are developed under the banner of didactics. Thus didactics is cross-cultural as a trend, yet its orientation leads us to understand curricula as forms given to local cultural exchanges: within the culture of the class, of the school, of this or that district, county, or state. The curriculum researchers and educators who have adopted the didactic approach also deal with issues of multicultural sensitivity. Didactics would be suited to the U.S. and Canadian contexts, as it specifically deals with the most sensitive current issues: how knowledge is built in communities; how curriculum is being created and communicated; what values and ethical issues influence the teacher-learner relationships; why educational standards – if they are to be proficiency based – will always be local, as they relate to local and culturally situated knowledge. U.S. readers are often resistant to ideas operating in another cultural setting – which *a contrario* is an indication that didactic thought is relevant in their settings.

Didactics seems almost unknown to the English-speaking world, though it constitutes a major movement in many non-anglophone countries. The emergent concept of didactics within the context of the European educational tradition has been presented on only two occasions at meetings of the American Educational Research Association, and presentations were focused on didactics in particular places (German-speaking countries, Hopmann, 1992; Scandinavia, Gundem, 1992; French-speaking countries, Tochon, 1999b). Research into and the practice of didactics are based on the premise that we can construct a pedagogy for each subject matter taught: a didactics of language, a didactics of mathematics, and so on. This conceptual movement rests upon very different assumptions than the field known as didactics in the United States two decades ago, and any old-fashioned associations that may cling to the English word *didactic* should be dismissed.

In its current form, didactics emphasizes the singularity of each teaching situation and attempts to integrate academic content with theories of education and pedagogy. Traditionally, specialists and designers of academic curricula have refused to consider pedagogy an object of interest; many researchers have tried to construct states-of-the-art for specific disciplines and subject matters without recourse to pedagogy (Bertrand & Houssaye, 1999). In contrast, didactic thought matches pedagogical needs to subject-matter knowledge. Each discipline is viewed through the lens of how it should be uniquely taught and learned; that is, how pedagogy should be enacted in particular disciplines because of the specific features of the subject matter. For this purpose, classroom interactions are studied in context to see how the signs and meaning of the subject are co-constructed and how the discipline is actualized into a particular pedagogy, into didaction.

The fifth chapter of this book is all about didaction. Didaction is a subtle concept, embedded in minute moves in teacher-learner encounters. Didaction is an expressive action in search of consistency; it develops indexical connections and relations with the socially useful aspects of creation and production. The didactive perspective situates education in the autonomous possibility of constructive emergence from the relation with others. In that context, evaluation becomes appraisal. Appraisal is the product and the process of creation or action, rather than the criteria-based anticipation of standards. Didaction offers a fresh denunciation of the instructional myth according to which it is possible to plan the representational course of others' learning. In contrast to this myth, didaction is a personal affair; it does not differ from the motivational choices of the individual. The examples of didaction provided here come from action poetry in the francophone world – Switzerland and Ontario – papering urban life with poems.

The afterword to this book turns to the social difficulties of those teachers who suffer from the Marshmallow Effect, allowing students to control the classroom. Demystifying teaching and teacher education is certainly not enough. It is an open door to Otherness. The afterword deals with education in competition with discourses on violence, within low-tier, high-security schools and boards of education, using Foucauldian metaphors and the gaze as foundational myths of security. The meaning of this exploration was renewed when the issue of who is terrorizing whom arose outside of education.

I would like to address the question of the larger context of this work. I refer to the work of other scholars, but Linda Rogers (personal communication, 2001) suggests that this book could be a part of a vigorous debate. This book is framed within a broad community of readers that extends beyond curriculum and instruction. Curiously enough, although narrative has an overwhelming presence in educational research, the field that developed narrative knowledge as its highest stake, semiotics, is almost entirely ignored in education (except in a small special interest group of the American Educational Research Association devoted to linking semiotics and education, which I chaired for three years). Conversely, this debate on narrative and deconstruction in education could be appealing to many scholars in the broader semiotic community, whose works are often published in the *International Journal of Applied Semiotics*.[1] A few years ago at AERA, there was a lecture by Jerome Bruner on narratives of experience, introduced by Ann Brown. Maybe three thousand educational researchers attended, many of whom had to sit on the floor, and a crowd was waiting outside. Most of Bruner's lecture was on the basics of semiotic inquiry and semiotic principles and analysis without using the name of semiotics, and nobody seemed to pay attention to this crucial, invisible link. Not one word was pronounced on semiotics as a field of study.

Semiotics is the all-permeating but ignored topic, as the average American reader does not seem to catch polysyllabic terms and words that require minimal reflection before handling (like *crusade*, for instance). Epistemology starts to be understood as a major issue if referred to with paraphrases like 'ways of knowing' rather than the specific word. Similarly, semiotics and its importance could easily be understood with simple examples, even in an almost analphabetic world where nuances and complexities that go beyond simple dualisms (for instance, the good ones against the bad ones) do not seem to be accessible to understanding. Danesi (1999b) made an extraordinary effort in that direction, choosing the appealing title *Of Cigarettes, High Heels, and Other Interesting Things.* He explained that any sign interpretation is a semiotic event embedded in a culture where this meaning is shared, as well as a series of contextualized representations of this meaning and events that are attached to it. Cigarettes and high heels are signs that stand for something other than themselves. Words that get meaning from contextualized features linked to their use are crucial to educational understandings. Semiotics is the sap of the educational flower; it is now time for semiotics to be recognized as one of the fundamental disciplines for education.

CHAPTER ONE

Myths in Teacher Education: Towards Reflectivity

Centuries ago in Mesoamerica, the Aztecs fought other coalitions in the name of beliefs preached by warrior-priests.[1] They killed thousands of prisoners, tearing out their living hearts to offer the bleeding, palpitating flesh to their gods. For the Aztecs, human sacrifice was a deeply sacred act, on which the whole continuation of the cosmos depended. In absolute contrast to this stood the Christian belief in God's love. For the Spanish invaders, human sacrifice was demonic work, and their belief gave them the conceptual energy and motivation to kill hundreds of thousands of indigenous people and served as a practical justification for the conquest of Mexico. They taught Christian love while praying for gold. Thus belief may serve as the pretext for war waged for economic expansion and power. Since the beginning of the human adventure, castes and groups have fought each other for power in the name of belief. Belief – note I do not say faith – has always served to divide people. Today, groups whose members come from many nations are still linked by discriminatory beliefs and act on human destiny by building boundaries, promoting elites in the supposed service of the powerless, and developing obedience systems very similar to those of ancient castes.

Systems of belief have always been the basis for directing masses of people, channelling their energy, and using it for profit. Education, paradoxically, is one such system. In ancient Greece, education was intended to distinguish and elevate each individual mind. However, this ideal, co-opted by mass schooling, is now the basis for moulding every mind to the same way of thinking. An analogy can be made to the way fashion has developed in relation to the body. Originally intended to individualize appearance and make the person unique (Barthes, 1967), fashion has become a mass system for making people resemble each other and conform to change, the way the countryside obeys the seasons. In a sense, education fashions the mind through current beliefs. Education is linked to explicit moral purposes; unlike the sculptor's studio it was in ancient Greece, it is a factory where minds are shaped to think the same way in the same circumstances.

In the name of an ideal and acting on belief, people have destroyed people; but also in the name of an ideal, people have loved each other, shared suffering, helped their neighbours – become one with or, indeed, transcended the human reality. And in the name of matter and materialism, people have destroyed people; but also in the name of matter, physicians have cured, cultivators have nourished, loving individuals have cared. Why do we need names when intention and action speak for themselves? In the Hebrew tradition, God's name is not to be spoken aloud. Muslims forbid representations of God's face. Brahmans have secret names for God. Our names delude where ideal and reality are concerned: they are facades that can hide palaces or slums. Idealistic names and materialistic names fashion a discourse that clothes the appearance of our actions and the flesh of our intentions.

It is now accepted that the same idea, the same word of wisdom, can be used to elevate or to destroy, depending on the intent behind it. Words have meaning in the context of action. They may conceal implicit targets and prevent the free development of the full potential for thought and action. Think, for example, of the use of euphemisms within professional communities. There is a belief that when reality is too crass, words should only allude. We learn to use uplifting words to formulate gentle, not to say sweet, descriptions of the bloody battles entailed by paradigm shifts and educational contradictions. Because fighting against a conceptual framework comes down to fighting with colleagues, thus threatening susceptibilities and challenging identities and beliefs; because fighting against a contradiction may endanger our own reputation; and because we are subject to the workings of networks of gossip, we fail to give voice to those feelings that differ from the shared beliefs of our caste. We don't express our shocked coming to awareness, but keep to what causes the least trouble. Members of a club, we refrain from telling our fellows that we oppose the abuse of a concept that was designed for a specific purpose for the bloodless accomplishment of its lethal contrary. Instead the way is paved for a move towards new concepts and tools by soft, delicate moves from right to left and from left to right, so that nobody will be shocked when we move – and so that when we move, the club moves with us.

In education, clubs are moved by doctrines built in common and by anxieties and self-protective measures all aligned with each other. Clubs are homes where we silently share contradictions. It is only when winds from outside, disturbing winds, dissipate the dark smoke of our polluted air, when we can no longer deny, that we acknowledge reality. Then for a while fresh air brings life and activity. But somehow life in a foggy club is easier than life in the lonely glare of enlightenment. That glare reminds us that protective networks are a mirage; that we are ever alone with our individual beliefs; that we will die solitary with the responsibility for our own intentions and actions.

Each club has its fashions and every club has its words. Science, arts, religion – welcome to the club. This chapter examines three educational clubs that shape beliefs in the field. My intention is not, through mere cynicism, to piss in my own backyard, as Kaestle (1993) puts it, but rather to point to shared facilities, or commonplaces. That stated truths cannot, by themselves, provide a moral education – for ourselves or for young people – is my concern. That mass educational concepts, even positive ones, can stifle individual growth, responsibility, and difference, is my worry. To this end, I will briefly describe three trends in teacher education and analyse them by deconstructing their discourse, looking for their inner contradictions. I will also add a moral, that is, a good intention wrapped in inadequate words, to do with the future of reflective trends in teacher education.

The first teacher-education discourse I will analyse is *mastery learning*, the discourse that uses the language of productivity, excellence, and efficiency. The second is *strategic teaching*, the discourse that targets expertise. The third is *narrative awakening*, the discourse of the enlightened subject. These three discourses belong to three educational clubs whose frames of reference correspond respectively to those of the ancient castes basic to any Indo-European society: workers, warriors, and priests.[2] It pleases me to think that these three castes work so nicely as metaphors for the three functional aspects of humanity addressed by these discourses. Productivity, warfare, and priesthood metaphorically shape three major trends in teacher education. The objective of my present quest for open-mindedness is their deconstruction. This chapter is engaged in a Howard Gardner–style (1993) fight against fraud; for caste discourse, though potentially motivating, is delusive.

History has shown that scientists resist refutation of their views. Kuhn (1962) argued that the goal of scientific explanation is to abstract confirmed data so that enough enigmas are produced to sustain the process of inquiry. The deductive methods of science rest on inductive inferential processes (Johnson-Laird & Byrne, 1991). The way these methods are usually presented, however, oversimplifies these processes and fails to take account of practical reality. Conversely, inductive approaches often fail to take account of the deductive dimension of some of the basic generalized rules that issue from implicit dogmatic postulates. Lack of refutability can lie hidden within both approaches. The stand I take in this chapter is that theories deployed in teacher education, even when partly wrong, have a motivational function. The degree of truth or falsifiability (Popper, 1974) to which educational models lay claim has little to do with any scientific validation; on the contrary, educational models appear to require a degree of unfalsifiability to be convincing. This will be shown in a thorough analysis of the three discourses introduced above. Deconstruction of all three models will provide a basis for proposing a postmodern, compatibilistic, conversational view of modelling and reflectivity in teacher education.

Mastery Learning, or the Business Caste

Goal-directed, performance-based education is not new. One generation ago, mastery learning promoted the desirability of unified goal definitions; expert-led definition of school tasks operating within a system assessing performance; curricular normalization and comparisons across communities, schools, and classes; standardized regulations; and clear expectations. Today, the standards movement rests on similar assumptions. Standardizing schooling and teacher education goes along with a trend that makes education a business. This may shift the locus of authority to external managers and turn teachers into instruments in the hands of quasi-corporate state authorities (Meier, 2000). As it may be difficult to take a historical stand on current trends, let us analyse how mastery learning managed the business metaphor.

Even though the myth of effectiveness is based on hard quantifications and numerical demonstrations, mastery learning is openly '*a philosophically based approach* to the design of classroom environments' (Block & Burns, 1976, p. 3, emphasis in original). The philosophy in question is that virtually *all people can learn well* under appropriate conditions of instruction. Teaching for mastery is meant to increase the chances for students' and teachers' *social survival* by dealing with basic intellectual competencies. School survival for all is an interesting communal concept whose optimism, which stands behind Carroll's model (1963, 1989), is in the true spirit of the Enlightenment and imbued with John Locke's theories of the perfectibility of human nature. This idea has been basic to recent commercials for schooling as a business activity. It invaded Great Britain and is now the standard for American education. For instance, *Business Week* proposed seven ways to fix America's schools. These 'ideas that work' are: pay teachers for performance, make schools smaller, hold educators accountable, offer more variety, provide adequate funding, increase time in school, and use technology effectively (Symonds, 2001, p. 67).

In the Indo-European tradition, the myth of the effectiveness of a collectivity was expressed in integrated ideals – or gods – responsible for large classes of society: people working in agriculture, those working in trade, collectivities unified in production. The gods of a caste expressed its conceptual framework, aggregates of concepts directly related to the day-to-day life of the members of that caste. These concepts, highly representative of the daily activities of commerce and agriculture, in turn motivated people to celebrate and enjoy their work and become effective. A late representative of this Indo-European tradition is the Roman god Quirinus, whose name comes from *co-virinus*, 'united force' (Dumézil, 1941). Quirinus was the god who brought together the energies of the caste of producers; the deification of pooled labour is deeply significant. Eventually, however, collective strength was translated into economic systems.

Similarly, an analysis of what has happened to the communal 'survival for all' spirit that animated mastery learning reveals that the logic of productivity defined by elapsed time, and its sequential regulation, has moved front and centre, with guaranteed minimal outcomes; meanwhile – in Carroll's words (1989) – the correspondence between quality of instruction and collective ability to understand instruction has been de-emphasized. That is, the philosophy of collective achievement seems to have been replaced by a more economically based notion of mass-produced profitability of outcomes. This business-style perspective seems to be the one advanced by the enterprising Yale/Harvard-based Gradgrindians who would see end-of-year examinations take place all across the United States. The standards movement is an inheritance from this philosophy of school efficiency (Sacks, 1999).

If we come down to pragmatic issues, however, results related to 'learning efficiency' can be quite misleading. Mastery learning methods from Carroll's mastery schools are based on efficiency in time. For Carroll (1963), student aptitude equates to the amount of time a student needs to learn the subject matter to a given level. Thus the level of learning from instruction is considered to be a linear function of the time spent learning as related to the time the student needed to spend. The now-famous linear equation, learning = F(time spent/time needed), is based on a purely sequential and administrative perspective of learning management. To use the terminology coined by anthropologist Edward Hall (1983), this is *monochronic* logic. In a system of production, monochronic rationales impose simplified, one-at-a-time decision-making processes. This kind of process typically does not fit easily into the natural complexity of the classroom (Hargreaves, 1989). In the shift from the promotion of a hedonistic philosophy of easy achievement for all to the espousal of the integration of simplistic rules for pacing instruction, mastery learning seems to have made a left-right move. The capital of future generations is now based on the timing of teaching and the measurement of contents, in order to attain wheat-from-chaff outcomes in a system of mass control. End-of-year examinations will screen children the way farmers choose cattle.

Well-defined objectives and formative evaluations were the primary components of mastery learning. According to the original version of this controversial instructional model, 95 per cent of pupils were intended to reach peak performance level (Bloom, Hastings, & Madaus, 1971). The process of working backwards from instructional objectives was a teacher-guided, top-down process, but evaluative regulations were required to provide bottom-up adaptive transformations to the instructional process itself. The most recent developments in the controversy still relate to the difficulty, in devising a forecast model, of anticipating the bottom-up changes to be made during the course of instruction. As early as 1976, Block and Burns had emphasized that, while the proponents of mastery learning assert that these approaches are flexible, its critics maintain mastery approaches are rigid and mechanistic. Ways to soften the monochronic sequencing of instruction have been studied under Bloom's guidance. Bloom (1984) presented two doctoral studies showing the standard deviations of outcomes between (A) normal classes (control group), (B) mastery learning classes, and (C) tutorial learning (one teacher per pupil, with some exceptions). The statistical difference among groups was one standard deviation. In statistics, one standard deviation – or *sigma* – is the variability index of one distribution. When distribution is normal, the standard deviation corresponds to a constant portion of the curve: about 68 per cent of observations for one sigma; about 95 per cent for two sigma. In the results that Bloom reported, the 'less good' student with a tutor (group C) had outcomes equal to or better than those of the best pupil in a normal class (group A). The 'mastery learning effect' (group B) gave average outcomes that were better than those of the best pupil in a normal class (group A). That is, the average outcome of mastery learning was one sigma better than control groups.

Bloom and his research team, however, wanted to reach a 'two-sigma effect.' Their goal was to obtain a tutorial-type result in a new, evolved, version of mastery instruction. To this end, they started analysing con-current variables that, once added to the well-defined objectives and formative evaluations, would provide outcomes superior by two sigma to those of normal, control-group classes (group A). The Chicago team, under Bloom's supervision, complicated the initial mastery model to such a point that one may wonder what, in education, *new wave* mastery learning would resemble. Emphasis in the literature on the supposed two-sigma effect can be explained by the fact that, while it is constantly said to be just around the corner, no instructional outcome has ever reached that peak. A difference of two standard deviations compared to control groups would suffice to claim mastery learning is the key approach to success for all; it would be the panacea of educational models. Mastery learning would be a practical applied philosophy enabling people to break out of underachievement, with practical as well as statistical validation.

One prediction made by Bloom was that mastery learning should lead 90 per cent of pupils to attain the achievement of the best 10 per cent. As Slavin (1987) has observed, to attain the two-sigma effect, nearly all pupils in a group would have to begin in the first centile and attain or exceed the criterial threshold of the ninetieth. The presence among them of even a few who began at the fiftieth centile, say, would defeat the two-sigma effect. In fact, the data suggest that mastery learning effects are far from reaching such homogeneity for all pupils in the same class. Major reviews and meta-analyses of studies on mastery learning show controversial results, far lower than the targeted two-sigma effect (Kulik, Kulik, & Bangert-Drowns, 1990). Guskey and Gates (1985) report highly positive effects of mastery instructional programs, with a mean of 0.78 standard deviation. But Slavin (1987) indicates that the results of those studies were biased and exaggerated. In any case, such meta-analyses are difficult to compare because of their limited field of application. Selection standards vary from review to review, and each adopts specific statistical procedures and unique ways of interpreting them. That is one reason why Kulik et al. conducted a meta-analysis of 108 studies on Bloom's mastery learning and the related Personalized System of Instruction (PSI). They obtained a standard deviation of 0.5 with control groups. This result, far lower than Bloom's guesses, is nevertheless superior to outcomes achieved with age-peer coaching (0.4), computer-assisted instruction (0.35), and 'open' education programs (–0.1), obtained with standardized testing.

In his response to the Kulik et al. meta-analysis, Slavin (1990) observed that the great majority of studies on mastery learning use non-standardized, experimenter-devised tests. In other words, these studies compare incomparables. Tests devised by experimenters seem to be biased in favour of mastery learning: they are built to measure the mastery program's objectives, whether or not these objectives were targeted by the control groups. For Robert Slavin, the effect of mastery learning outcomes as measured by standardized tests is nil; using non-standardized measurements, he finds it to be weak (0.25) and biased. To help move the debate 'out of the unproductive proponent-critic mode,' Burns (1992) outlined three areas in need of research in the field of mastery learning: aptitude, time, and outcome. He observed that the conceptual distinction between aptitude and achievement had been 'cloudy at best' (p. 11). While short-term achievement operates in a bottom-up direction, long-term ability operates top-down and facilitates future success. But the differential correspondence between quality of instruction and ability to understand it is as imprecise as the Vygotskian optimal level of learning. Burns remarks, 'unfortunately, these ideas have never been tested well' (ibid.). Moreover, differential effects in learning time and quality of instruction are in his view questionable and uncertain. The negative consequences of providing too much support to students of high ability have not been questioned. But just this point has been raised in classroom practice, where repeated formative evaluations have been found to be boring and demotivating. Using language based on maximizing benefits with faster outcomes, critics of mastery learning question whether the higher achievement is worth the additional time required. Practical questions remain unsolved by the mastery model: How long does the teacher wait for slow students? What to do with faster students? As regards outcomes, the rallying cry that Bloom's mastery model would erase individual differences is acknowledged by both Carroll (1963) and Burns to be more of a slogan than a statement of truth. Ultimately, they point out, the desirability of a model's outcomes and dispersion derives from value judgments.

As well, Burns (1992) articulates basic criticisms of the research economy upholding mastery models. Most mastery research has evaluated school implementation. Control groups were not involved and data were 'typically spotty and ambiguous' (p. 21). Furthermore, the interpretation of results was often political and did not conform to scientific standards. Experimental and quasi-experimental research done on mastery learning was of short duration, with researcher-based materials and measures, eliminating the teacher-effect of real class experience and overestimating the effects of variables studied. In the rare field experiments, control was sacrificed to pragmatic purposes and random selection of teachers was most often replaced by volunteering. In brief, basic precautions to secure the credibility of results in this experimental paradigm were rarely taken. It is, then, not surprising that Burns notices a 'considerable confusion over mastery learning' (p. 16); examples of such confusion are unintended deviations from the mastery regimen and 'poor and unimaginative interpretations of mastery learning' (ibid.). That is, the execution of the mastery learning concept is based on interpretations of a rallying cry, whose motivational slogans are based on beliefs presented unfalsifiably as evidence. Burns (1992) ends his study by saying that the ultimate goal of mastery-learning research is to understand the effects of instruction on groups of learners rather than to debate whether their mean effect is 'nil' or 'two-sigma.'[3]

To summarize, within the mastery learning paradigm, students' ability is equated to learning time. In this view, mastery should occur given enough time, support, and scaffolding with feedback. Under these conditions, mastery learning procedures are expected to yield learning gains that approximate two standard deviations. This expectation is purportedly supported by experimental evidence demonstrating exceptional learning results. It appears, however, that control groups are often evaluated using assessment instruments specially designed for the mastery learning situation, but not the control group situation. Moreover, using the two-sigma standard deviation as a criterion for mastery entails a complete shift from almost no knowledge to full knowledge among all students in a year. Such a result might have some probability of occurring in first grade, assuming that pupils were 'tabula rasa' entering elementary school. But what about the second or third grades? The 'evolution' of mastery learning towards more refined variables to enhance success becomes so complex that the model could become impractical, if not impossible, for teachers to handle in actual school settings. In any case the validity of this approach continues to rest on the two-sigma hypothesis, which, as pointed out above, is founded on a basic contradiction (and as Slavin [1987] points out, it is fraught with methodological problems). This contradiction is at the heart of the web of contradictions that pervade the mastery learning research paradigm as it is proposed in teacher education.

These details are important because they reveal the mythic background of an influential educational paradigm. Although proponents of this economic approach have an interest in maintaining people's belief that the mastery model is homogeneous, in reality the model embraced an unstable multiplicity of constantly re-examined variables. It is intriguing to observe that the theory of mastery learning has been partly invalidated on the grounds that were used to legitimize its outcomes: experimental standards and statistics. Moreover, the two-sigma effect is derived from parametric measurements that should be theoretically incompatible with 'J curves' of mastery achievement.

The mastery learning approach still thrives in teachers' colleges and school settings (L.W. Anderson, 1996; Guskey, 1994; Sacks, 1999; Solway, 1999; Waddington, 1995). The new state-mandated standards are but an *excroissance* of the mastery framework. The leitmotif of meritocracy hides the fact that many people are not given the chance to keep up with the imposed standards (Meier, 2000). Some women and minorities have even embarked on the standards boat, hoping it might make a difference: same standards to master for all, with common goals and common tests. Everybody will work in the same direction. Notwithstanding, we may wonder whether this will simply drive us all from work slavery to human robotization: everyone has to think alike, behave alike. The reward system guides the masses towards blind obedience and acceptance of what the leadership dictates. This mastery appears suspicious. Outcomes-based education and performance assessment are the source of this trend, and they now spread out all around at a state level. Should we then reject this model? Not at all. Even though evaluation is a real danger for individual freedom because it classifies social strata, and evaluation is so reductive that it cannot grasp the higher levels of learning, its imperfections may prevent some of its most cruel abuses. People feel good speaking the language of standard assessment; politicians will be glad, and the public will think something has been done to improve the educational system.

The first role of teacher educators would seem to be to conceptually homogenize heterogeneous research outcomes. Bloom's rallying-cry was in perfect alignment with that role. The second role of teacher educators would seem to be to contextualize educational models in terms that fit practitioners' needs. If educators and teachers have adopted mastery learning with beneficial results in their own particular context, then it must provide a motivational framework to help thinking-about-practice improve practice. In other words, the de facto validity of successful classroom experiences seems a more convincing basis for adopting the model than the validity of statistical measures. The critical reflections that teacher educators share with practitioners about the relationship of the ideal and the real in mastery learning appear to be a good way to enhance practice by providing motivational interactions. Does it matter if mastery learning is a myth? If performance assessment is a good intention packaged in the discourse of business? The model was made so convincing that people enjoyed the business metaphor of managing their classes' productivity, following the rules for productivity in business. The metaphor was born among teachers and educators, and motivated them. Does it really matter if the experimental 'proofs' were questionable? The important thing was that people *thought* it was rigorous. The perception of rigour makes people think and act rigorously at a time when such thinking is felt useful. In the last analysis, the motivational effects are perhaps more important than the so-called two-sigma effect or the standards themselves. But remember: this is only the bottom educational caste.

Strategic Teaching, or the Warrior Caste

The warrior caste is the second one on the scale. The word *strategy*, already in use among behaviourists, has been integrated into cognitive problem-solving. It should surprise no one that stimulus-response concepts were transferred to condition-action rules of symbolic approaches in the cognitive sciences. In technical terms, a given cognitive procedure is a condition-action rule (*if ..., then ...*). A strategy can be defined as a heuristic system, that is, a chain of condition-action rules that allows one to reach a complex goal B from a situation A through a problem-space AB (Newell & Simon, 1972). Activation of some procedures may spread through the whole network of cognitive rules in search mode. This is referred to as the spreading activation of procedural knowledge.

Problem-solving strategies have been studied in learners, and as cognitive psychology has become increasingly interested in complex learning environments, research on teaching has begun to be conducted in terms of problem-solving strategies. In both cases, light is being shed on both simple, algorithmic chains and the heuristic strategies needed in more complex situations.

Strategic teaching emerged in the field of curriculum and instruction from the synthesizing work of a team (Jones, Palincsar, Ogle, & Carr, 1987) whose goal was twofold: 1) to suggest ways of teaching thinking and thinking strategies; 2) to transfer to teacher education the results of cognitive research on learning as applied to content areas. Strategic teaching appeared at a time when cognitive research seemed mature enough to inform method courses in teacher education. The cognitive community had already established a common framework relating instruction to cognitive research (Segal, Chipman, & Glaser, 1985). Cognitive education was modelled with clear guidelines and a theory (Marzano et al., 1988). This declarative 'truth' indicated how important transfer (through procedural knowledge) was. In cognitive psychology, transfer is defined as the decontextualization of knowledge such that it can be applied in a new context. Transfer is accomplished by decontextualizing knowledge to apply its (meta)components to new fields of discovery.

Although some aspects of research on teacher thinking have been integrated into research on student thinking, the model of 'cognitive pedagogy' provides an idealized and decontextualized view of a teacher who intervenes at the levels of content, cognitive, and metacognitive strategies; gives clear information on the most appropriate strategies for reaching a target; helps construct knowledge and organize student knowledge through schemata; and explicitly informs students of their responsibility to engage themselves in the task with motivation by taking on attainable challenges. Based on this initial model, program directors and school superintendents joined forces, anxious to implement higher-level thinking skills in the classroom. They soon generalized the new approach, though research results on teaching transfer and interdisciplinary strategies were rather unconvincing (Weinstein, Goetz, & Alexander, 1988). At least sixty-four reputable university teachers endorsed a strategic teaching model, and it was promoted in well-received books (Jones & Idol, 1990; Resnick & Klopfer, 1989). It has been claimed by the journal *Educational Leadership* that strategic teaching became dominant at the beginning of the nineties. Strategic teaching was winning the war against other models of instruction, such as mastery learning, despite basic unsolved questions.

Among the questions left unsolved by strategic teaching proponents are:

1 whether it is possible to teach thinking strategies;
2 how to resolve the confusion between cognitive and metacognitive strategies;
3 the nature of metacognition; and, above all,
4 how to transfer the model to teacher education programs and actual classrooms.

We will take each of these four questions in turn, although they are closely linked.

The possibility of teaching thinking strategies has been questioned by research on heuristics and on interdisciplinary 'use your head' courses for underachievers. Basic to the teaching of strategies is a profound understanding of what a mental strategy might be. Reading the literature on cognitive and metacognitive strategies, one can have the feeling that many authors are unaware of the full implications of what they have shown, namely, that strategies are not simple cognitive internalization of behaviours (Vygotsky's stand was more subtle). Rather, they are made of the material of thought; their own substance is thought. Thus there arises the erroneous hypothesis that teaching words that represent inferred strategies will enhance levels of thinking. To support this position, much research has enumerated the frequencies of various strategies. When these are more closely examined, it becomes evident that, though definitions are provided for each strategy, the process of distinguishing them in learners' thinking is highly inferential. Any researcher who has spent a few weeks coding verbal protocols, whether concurrent or retrospective (Ericsson & Simon, 1994), needs no convincing of this. Piaget (1974) is perhaps easier to apply, with his distinction between 'reflecting abstraction' (implicit and unexpressed) and 'reflective abstraction.'

Even the clear statements of Garner (1987) about the expressibility of metacognition appear unconvincing after a few weeks of strategic coding. Just take McKeachie's definitions (McKeachie, Pintrich, Lin, & Smith, 1988) of cognitive and metacognitive strategies and notice how, with further thought, cognitive strategies look very metacognitive in the last analysis; suddenly you no longer know what metacognition means. See, for example, the 'revision' process that McKeachie et al. attributed to cognitive strategies. Have you ever seen good revision without control? In what conditions? Perhaps in conditions where revision has been used so many times in the same context that it became automatic. However, the first times you revise a new task, shouldn't it be clearly defined as a metacognitive process? This example provides evidence that 'cognitive pedagogy' has not dealt with some basic issues well-known to behavioural researchers, such as the push-down principle. The push-down principle indicates that complex tasks become simpler and more automatic with habit, and move down the taxonomy of thinking skills.

Will you teach strategy A, just because it is in the K-3 program, to a child for whom it has been routine for two years? And what if a child has developed more efficient but unknown strategies, or the most efficient strategies for succeeding in school without effort – that is, unethically – strategies for *not* learning (Buckley & Cooper, 1978; Perrenoud, 1988)? Clearly, metacognition is not like a set of nested boxes that everyone can access at an equal pace. It is an interpretation of mental reality, based upon a modern conceptual framework that cuts the subject off from his or her mental objects. Metacognition presumes that human beings can transcend their condition-action rules and grasp their control processes at a level of pure awareness. In philosophy, this way of thinking has been labelled *subjective idealism.* In contrast, postmodern philosophy argues that higher levels of meaning are always embedded in a complex of nested values. Since meaning is situated, it cannot be grasped without reference to its interconnections with situations. The postmodern stance presumes the impossibility of metaknowledge. Postmodern teacher education is, for the time being, unclassified. Perhaps its adherents correspond to outcastes, rising up with touchy, untouchable questions. The Pandora's box of metacognition is heir to five millennia of Indo-European speculation – stay with me and I'll come back to this question.

In strategic teaching, the role of different types of knowledge in information processing is emphasized. Declarative knowledge is said to answer the question of what knowledge is needed for a task and to fix factual data. Declarative data are said to be static; invoking the metaphor of artificial intelligence, it could be said that they are stored in long-term memory. These data have to be pinpointed and reprocessed to be transformed into action. Conversely, procedural knowledge is said, in the literature on reading, to answer questions about the 'how' of a task (Winograd & Hare, 1988). On this point there seems to be confusion between the questions that must be asked in order for experts to build production systems and the procedural part of a condition-action rule. Since the three types of knowledge (declarative, procedural, and conditional) are constitutive of any condition-action rule, they are part of any action. Telling teachers to develop these three types of knowledge does not translate into anything other than normal behaviour as far as the student is concerned.

Condition-action spreading activation is capable of great flexibility and occurs in parallel with other types of processes. In what Bereiter (1991) called new symbolic-connectionist networks, mental models may process aspects of stored information as condition components (*if*) of procedures, while the action components of the procedural rules (*then*) may be connected by pointers to various items of reprocessed stored information, according to variability evaluations of the action's targets in the environment (Holland, Holyoak, Nisbett, & Thagard, 1986). Mental models seem far more flexible than schemata. They are not grounded in typical events but rather in the restructuring of the knowledge of events to fit situated information and to create exception-rules. In theory, mental models evaluate and adapt to competing information and account for atypical situations, but this does not seem to be the case when the schema theory is applied in strategic teaching.

Strategic teaching inherits the metaphoric use of McClelland and Rumelhart's (1988) and J.R. Anderson's (1983) concepts from the literature on reading, in which types of knowledge are defined in terms of their roles (what, how, when) despite the fact that cognitive literature negates the viability of those semantic roles in pragmatic contexts (Clancey, 1992; Whitson, 1992). Although Marzano (1991) tries to correct this trajectory by giving curricular definitions that are closer to work in cognitive science, the description he provides remains schematic. Conceptual models used by researchers to describe their results are already in some ways metaphoric transpositions of reality. Even for a scientist, there is no evidence other than what one sees in one's own mind. By the time these transpositions are in turn transposed into teacher education frameworks, metaphors have attained the status of beliefs. The cautious language of scientific acceptance has been simplified to suit the grasp of people who have no knowledge of the theory's foundational epistemology.[4]

In the case of strategic teaching, a major transposition has been made from the concepts of cognitive psychology into a teachable framework. The words are used and reused in such a way that they are banalized, made trite, and the original metaphors are lost. But it is sufficient to watch a military exercise on TV to grasp the extent to which predetermination is bound up in the metaphor of strategy. It leads people to believe that the solution has been found – or at least that a problem-solving strategy is being implemented. Who decides the nature of the problem in this model? Who decides the strategy? Instead of leaving the pupils free with their own mental strategies, we teach them. The risk then arises of subtle indoctrination regarding the *manner* of thought. Strategies to be followed are described so precisely that the pupils can no longer reflect but must rather reproduce the strategies dictated, on which they are evaluated. Once upon a time we taught children logical argument. Today we teach them to place a connector or a transitional phrase at the start of each paragraph but nowhere else. There is no longer any subtlety in reason; the very fact of isolating strategies from their context entails reductionism.

There is a danger that teaching thinking becomes teaching a child to think the way one wants the child to think. Like soldiers, children taught this way will learn to think strategically, that is, to respond quickly in terms of task-effectiveness, but with no regard to the underlying framework that makes a task significant or aberrant. Whereas encyclopedic models of teaching fed students various sorts of knowledge to the point where the more 'use your head' educators feared manipulative indoctrination, now the prevailing emphasis is on everybody using the same strategies to fit the correct goals. Strategies and targets are supplied; the rest is a matter of discovery. This yields excellent mind warriors, but directed in their way of thinking: the structure of their way of thinking is manipulated from their youth. Encyclopedic education engaged the mind in a plurality of contents – contents that could be manipulative – but processing was left free. Children could choose their own ways to consume all that food for thought. Now fast foods are moulded to fit into condition-action boxes, and no time is left to think.

The contents of the black box have long been neglected by behaviourists: in their view there was evidence only of pre-minded behavioural stimuli and post-minded behavioural responses, with no depiction of the inside, of the mind. Cognitive research has aimed to remedy this situation: it opened the Pandora's box of cognition, trying both to see what's inside and to fill it up with concepts, attitudes, procedures, strategies, and so on. The idea of strategies gives a feel for the inside, for the mind, but when teaching a child to feel or fill or feed the box with condition-action rules (strategies or chains of procedures), *we forget that the target of these strategies is imposed.* While there is some reflection on the process, there is no reflection on the target; we teach teachers how to train strategic learners who could accept any content as long as they govern their mental strategies properly – useful future soldiers for a mechanical society.

The moral of this somehow tragic strategic story is that mass education rests upon metaphors and beliefs, however informed and scientific and elevated the original intentions may have been. Because only human-to-human relationships can deeply penetrate the educational fibre, mottoes will remain mind tools, used by some individuals for the better but by others for the worse. Transcending the Manichaeism of modernity – although postmodernity does not transcend – we may say things are neither white nor black. Thus, seeking deconstructive aspects of strategic teaching in order to point the mind towards future reconstructible untargets, we may advance the discussion and examine the contradictions of this model as regards teacher education.

Adaptive, flexible planning was basic to the stance taken by strategic teaching: bottom-up information obtained in the pedagogical field was to be taken into account. That is, the situatedness of modelling was emphasized (Tochon, 1999a). Since we now know that knowledge is distributed in the environment, it is easy to guess the problems encountered by unsituated forecasting models (Bibby, 1992). Open, bottom-up planning models, however, immediately posed problems in turn. How do we plan for the unforeseen? Moreover, the effort to transfer to teacher-education models a set of results that had emerged from research on strategic learning in itself contradicted the premises of flexible, open planning. As the research on didactic transposition shows, the transfer of knowledge to the field of teacher education entails a stage of reductive homogenization of knowledge such that it is removed from its initial context of research (Chevallard, 1999). As with any transfer, the transposing of research results was made possible by decontextualizing research knowledge for the purpose of generalizing educational models. Nobody asked who was to be responsible for recontextualizing that knowledge. The teacher was therefore left alone to navigate by the stars in a sea of contexts, with strategic mottoes as a rudder and students' reactions as a sail. Was that so different from previous instructional designs and mastery models?

Thus, teachers were repeatedly advised to take students' representations into account; but who, among strategic educators, could claim that this new strategic knowledge was built on teachers' prior representations? The metatransfer role of knowledge of teaching did not play a part in the vision of strategic education. While aware of the decontextualizing nature of transfer, proponents of strategic thinking did not seem to evaluate its inevitable consequences when translating their models into generalized beliefs. Thus, the transfer of results from research on learning to teacher education implied its decontextualization. The paradox here is that strategic results designed by researchers had to be modelled by teacher educators so as to be remodelled by teachers, who in turn showed learners how to model their own learning. There were at least three successive phases of transfer, that is, a meta-meta-decontextualizing of knowledge. Who spoke up about situated cognitions for teacher education courses?

The fact is that curriculum implementation of strategic thinking did not seem to consider research on the other aspect of transfer, school change (Gambone & Connell, 1998). Bottom-up models learned during teacher education were applied top-down. Educators often treat concepts as if they were rigid and stable entities. But in the field of cognition it is not possible to proceed this way: cognitions derive from subtle processes that are difficult to give an account of with only rallying cries bolstered by rational arguments intended to ensure correct, uniform interpretation in relation to every child. One way to break out of vicious circles of transfer could, of course, be to try avoiding teachers' inference and directly study the effects of instructional programming on cognitive strategies, or directly study teachers' cognitive strategies as they fit the practical needs of students. Peer coaching may be a solution. But words won't become pure cognitions, and there will always be variability in what cognitive concepts represent operationally among various researchers, educators, and teachers.

Meanwhile, instructional models that tend to suppress the teacher cannot go far in supporting learners' development. Certain kinds of motivational information, information about confidence in the path and the goal, are not provided by computers and peers. When a small group of learners is plugged into a hypertext network without human guidance, the results do not seem very convincing. Viens (1991) observed K5–6 pupils creating a data bank. In collaborative hypertext writing, children seemed unable to define keywords and incapable of linking various items of knowledge. They either did not index or they performed negative indexations; in other words, they either didn't link items of knowledge to each other or else they established incorrect conceptual relations among contents. Sure, the children improved at selecting keywords, but they were soon fed up with the machine, with their failure to learn new words, and with the overuse of dictionary files. The idea that learning can be directly developed without developing teaching seems to be another myth.

It also seems debatable that one could educate teachers without having a practical knowledge of the classroom, their field of operations. The learning strategies identified through research on thinking are quasi-general. The teacher is the person to adapt adaptive models and make words fit experience. Research provides models and conceptual orientations, which then must be recontextualized by those onto whose shoulders they are transferred. Such details are revealing, providing a backstage view of an important educational prop. Specialists in transfer have forgotten that they are transferring knowledge in a decontextualized way. Again, it is highly interesting to note that the strategic thinking trend is partly invalidated just because it does not stick to its own premises.

Becoming an educated person depends upon one's own industry (as mentioned on the frontispiece of London's New College; Meier, 2000, p. 81). But uniformity is the pathway. School bureaucracy will not change class size, proven to be a major factor in learning inequities: it will emphasize standards and control at a lesser cost. In the same way that mastery learning contradicts its own experimental premises, strategic teaching does not take into account some basic features of its own active principle: the nature of cognition and transfer were not fully grasped, nor were the risks involved in the decontextualization of knowledge. But teachers came to be – and still are – motivated by strategic beliefs. Is it important that the model was contradictory, when these partly applicable, paradoxical language games engendered true enthusiasm among teachers, educators, and researchers? If teachers adapt these concepts with beneficial results and enjoy them in their context, it is probably because this framework helps them reflect on their practice and improve it. Attempts at adaptation and recontextualization among these teachers might well be as formative a practice as the declarative knowledge they have received about learning strategies.

Narrative Autobiography, or the Priestly Caste

Originally intended for purposes of biographical research in the tradition of the Chicago school, verbal protocols from teachers on their lives and experiences have been useful in various ways during the last decade. The progressive shift in the way life stories are applied might be described as an evolution of perspective from researcher-oriented to teacher-oriented (Zay & Day, 1998). This shift corresponds to the evolution within the educational research community from a modern view of research, as intended to discover and analyse structural patterns and correspondences between multicase or single-case verbal protocols, to a postmodern view of research as a collaborative, nonhierarchical inquiry initiating a conversation between the teacher and the other. The other, in the emerging conversational inquiry, may be a peer-teacher, a peer-coach, a supervisor, or an academic researcher. While discussing teacher stories in terms of verbal protocols and their use makes for a researcher-oriented interpretation, research in the educational sciences in general has become increasingly phenomenological over the years. That is, more emphasis has been placed on developing a reflection on experience, sharing definitions of the practitioner as a person who interacts with various contexts, and building perspectives and shared representations on the lived environment. Thus the priestly caste looks more democratic and humanistic, and would seem to be the one place where women and minorities can express their voices. On the other hand, it is still a male-dominated setting, where only authorized voices prevail. Nonetheless the narrative church contains some safe places where community feelings can start to grow, among caring voices.

Whether in a researcher-oriented or more teacher-oriented context, biographical stories certainly helped to bring research and theory closer to practice and academic teachers closer to their colleagues' real problems at the pre-school, elementary, and secondary levels. Biographical stories help teachers in reflecting and acting in their context with a clear intentionality (Cochran-Smith & Lytle, 1999). Indeed, reflective and reciprocal verbalizations have a critical value in reorganizing the way one thinks about a topic. The shift from research goals to teacher goals is reflected in the way journals are increasingly used to express teachers' practical concerns directly, rather than being mediated through structural analyses. Teachers' involvement in research has thus increased.

The parallel, increased involvement by researchers in teachers' lives and concerns may be explained by a variety of factors. For example, after a decade of research on innovation, it appeared clear that top-down innovations did not work. A range of bottom-up innovations had to be integrated into practice, and teacher representations therefore had to be taken into account. Then, trends in teacher innovation merged with concerns about teacher knowledge. Another synthesis is the progressive merging of narrative and critical approaches within a sociocultural framework. Nowadays the usefulness of research is often related to change, intervention, and policy. Researchers are perhaps more cautious about the role their research plays in the political interplay of obedience systems – systems that impose roles and hierarchies according to ways of thinking. Researchers seem increasingly aware of the doctrinal aspects and power perspectives that explain research models, interpretations, and discourse.

What approach could be more deeply entrenched in situational, lived events than narrative biography? Language provides meaning and the sense of 'I'-ness to journal-keeping practitioners and to the readers who share their experiences, in a way that probably makes their construals act directly upon further classroom situations (Connelly & Clandinin, 1995). Narrative sharing becomes networking (Russell, Mawhinney, Banks, & Ortiz, 1998), because it's a treat to share devices that work. For a long time the reductionism of tricks and recipes in education was decried. Some people even would have had us believe that teacher education of the time consisted in learning a set of gimmicks that call Disneyworld to mind. Gimmicks were therefore banished, and didactic engineering was established on a scientific basis, so that it might be taken seriously (Lacotte & Lenoir, 1999). And yet, following this period of banishment, the tricks and recipes of teaching are coming back into favour, as teacher educators happily acknowledge their worth: they serve as instruments for reflection and have inductive, hermeneutic value. Currently, using narrative research on the slices of life represented by these tricks and recipes, an effort is being made to package them using case studies and vignettes. Banks of cases are being built up, with their true-life contents capable of flexible adaptation to varied educational contexts so that teacher reflection on practice can be elicited. This new view of teacher education points to renewed credibility for the practical, a new face in practice.

Consequently, biographical inquiry and approaches to the personal, as expressed in the vast, ongoing conversation on teacher vignettes, cases, and stories, seem far more rooted in complex classroom realities than mastery and strategic approaches to teacher education. The mediation between research and education is diminished, and researcher biases should also be lessened – as regards teachers' views, at least. Researchers had been accused of being incomprehensible. With the shift towards phenomenology, the use of ordinary vocabulary makes their work more accessible and their research accounts more responsive to the questions of practitioners. At the same time, the problem of ensuring ecological validity for research is resolved. The new readability should also serve as 'answerability,' as called for by exponents of narrative methods. In classical terms, in shifting from the structures of meaning to the flesh of incarnate experience, educational inquiry certainly gained much validity but probably lost some reliability.

Those classical terms are at the crux of the shift from a modern to a postmodern use of the narrative in teacher-education research. Whereas some narrative researchers try to retain safeguards with respect to the norms and codes of modern educational science research, other researchers propose a different perspective, in which Bruner's (1990) 'verisimilitude' would appear to suffice as a scientific consideration; that is, the reasonableness and seeming fidelity of a story to the realities of the field suffice to make it instructive for change. This argument, at the boundary between art and science, becomes central in the debate over the creation of a lore of praxis and indicates some crucial limitations to the narrative approach.

The motto of teacher educators who embrace this approach is freedom and autonomy. Indeed, there is a current convergence of views between narrative and critical educators. Empowering others, they become stars by giving others a voice (Chandler, 1992). But this paradigm also subjugates disciples and indicates what wrong thinking to avoid. It suggests what to think and how to teach, and points the masses down the path of righteous autonomy. Researchers working in this trend stipulate what is right to do and think, and extrude moral profiles of the good teacher. But soon enough their sterile leitmotifs co-opt the isolated voices floating upwards, into a communitarian but top-down discourse, codified by those who have the right to say what must be thought in this field, those who hold the real power to speak. People cease thinking, overwhelmed by the whole journal-keeping enterprise. The focus on the self is great, but there's no time left for students: teachers, educators, researchers are all engaged in self-development. Autonomy has become a paradoxical tool for indoctrination and manipulation. The epitome of the anti-method, once it is elevated to the status of ultimate method, becomes a system of constraint implying rigid norms and an obedience to (again) exclusive truth.

Narrative builds its doctrine on its own, negating two of its main sources: sciences and the arts. This emancipation becomes problematic when the historical reasons for earlier safeguards in the use of story are not attended to. Indeed, teacher story telling appears historically detached from common definitions of narrative arts and the science of history; its anarchical use in teacher education, if severed from this earlier knowledge, might contribute to a paradoxical narrative absolutism (I will develop this point in chapter 2). The educational community is currently witnessing a synchronic narrativism, dehistoricized by being removed from its past in the search for increased awareness. As for the arts, educational story does not fit aesthetic purposes and research. Thus, this paradoxical, antidiachronic, unaesthetic story making acquires its relevance in a depth-psychology approach to teaching. It could even be claimed to be post-structural; in the absence of a frame of reference, it is a moving conceptual framework. It is becoming a mythic whole consisting of a maze of mottoes, supervised by the invisible mentors who are proponents of the upcoming 'best thing' to believe in (Latour, 1996).

Detached from the arts and from science, narrative is developing a growing body of rites and litanies that people are led to repeat in chorus. Its fluency makes the narrative trend susceptible to manipulation from above, by people interrelated in a way that helps them control the myths that the masses are to subscribe to. The principles of the narrative approach have become hegemonic in recent years. Their consecration risks reinforcing the ties of dependency between practitioners and certain educators, whose professional justification is nevertheless bound up specifically with the negation of the very obedience links they create. These obedience links are then conceptually justified in the terms of emancipation. Enlightenment and freedom are promoted through methods of control. When liberation is defined as a reimagining of one's story, we are approaching political generalizations. (In the Paris of May 1968 the slogan 'The beach lies under the pavement' could be read sprayed on walls while students tore up the pavement and threw pieces of it at anti-demonstration clones. It was then a message of deliverance. This slogan, intended to evoke the spirit of freedom associated with holidays by the sea and contact with nature and to decry the paved rigidity of the economic overlay on this spirit, has now been co-opted by Club Med advertisements.)

Narrative consumerism has been amplified in recent years. Many admit it is building a metanarrative. In epitaphic style, and duly maintaining their dominant position, some teacher educators epitomize a narrative approach that would persist in the goal of teacher enlightenment. Their Fodor to guided awakening reveals how a humanist effort may pass from guidance to the creation of dependency. Holding their students' hands as the students advance to the next stage of further possible retellings, they admit their reluctance to push too hard and acknowledge how much risk is involved in relationships of trust. There is some loneliness in the ivory tower of initiation, when one feels representative enough of a trend not to refer to others any more (Magnusson, 1999). For instance, when the Promised Land cannot be reached without conflict, some teacher educators blame the loss of supporters, storying fatigue, and diverse traumas associated with secular priesthood. Change cannot occur without catharsis. Reformulations of restories do not always restore autonomy to followers. What some specialists even consider to be narrative onanism certainly involves self-satisfaction, textual pleasure, but it does not change reality much.

One of the analytical procedures used by teacher educators in this context consists of deconstructing the role of hero in a personal narrative, which always takes a prominent place, often at the expense of other partners in the story; the teacher educator seeks to disentangle the strands in teachers' tales of influence by their students (Clandinin & Connelly, 1996). However, it remains true that the educator himself or herself is caught up in analogous mechanisms. Those who guide the process of awakening cannot themselves break out of the romantic role of saviour, and they produce norms of conduct through their interpretations of others' fantasies. Narrative search has turned into therapy (Monk, Winslade, Crocket, & Epston, 1997). Restories, shared in groups and forming cultural entities, build a Narrative Dream. But oneiric language may put one's critical faculties to sleep; the language of initiation may serve as a Castaneda-style dose of peyote – the belief that one is leaping out of reality whereas in fact one is building one's own prison of words. Even words of wisdom may imprison. Hope can be exploited to the point where countless people are persuaded to wear out their bottoms with yogic flying in their expressed desire to overcome their students' problems. The exploitation of hope is fraud, and story making can become deception. At a time when universities make money from teachers, this risks becoming a swindle. To hoax teachers, sing the virtues of day-dreaming. Any new discourse will fit.

In a society where everybody is meant to think positively, initiation certainly no longer resides in the use of metaphors and phonemes, nor in the advice to stop thinking. Initiation, in the sense of a beginning, may be found in the move towards looking for what one thinks that is different from what anybody else is thinking. It would seem doubtful that anyone could or should tell another person when and how this 'othernessing' process should start. This is a private decision, with hard consequences. As expressed in the prephenomenological assumptions of objective idealism (Harland, 1987), the expression of the private life in stories may hide the nature of experience with a curtain of words. The same words may refer to numerous inner dramas. In the narrative dream, initiation and awakening have been scenarized. For example, Connelly and Clandinin use the parable of a narrow ridge, borrowed from Buber's community of otherness. This 'place of tension between gulfs' 'allows the possibility of overcoming otherness' (1990, p. 5). But the ridge is a dangerous place: it is easy to fall off into the gulf that nearly surrounds you. Now it is as if every teacher must cross an imaginary river, while educators are the indispensable boatmen who can take them across. All this is only human.

As Gomez and Tabachnick (1992, p. 8) write, 'telling stories, even good stories, does not by itself lead to development as a teacher.' Accomplishments in story are embedded in the tyranny of words. 'Narratives that promote coherence, singularity and closure, and which aim to set up a cosy camaraderie with the reader, are ultimately conservative and uncritical of prevailing ideological and representational arrangements. If we refuse to interrogate these forms, we run the risk of promoting an uncritical research practice which, in seeming to describe teachers as they really are, simply perpetuates ... iconographies of teacher-hood.' (MacLure & Stronach, 1992, p. 21).

The arguments of educators in the narrative school can be misleading. Theoreticians decry the abuse of theory and use the essay to promote the 'non-theoretical form of discourse' of narrative; stories become 'convivial critical theories' to 'reverse the decline of the public imagination' (Barone, 1992a, p. 11–12). Enlightened proselytism brings a vast public to share those ideal visions. Academicians are encouraged to intervene in public conversations in an 'emancipatory-minded discourse' (p. 4). The liberatory aspect of narrative appears crucial when it aims at social change. Critical storytelling 'openly asserts human emancipation as a guiding value'; it is 'meant to demystify' (p. 4). However, as the French philosopher Alain Finkelkraut has said, nowadays, for a myth to have any chance of enticing people it must wear the appearance of demystification. Recent research on truth telling in narrative reflections suggests that student teachers feel they are taught to lie in reporting stunning experiences and raising of consciousness (Tochon, 2002a).

Towards a Reflective Mythology

It may be ironic that current school administrations have reached the peak of what the caste system may offer: mass thinking and unification of all under one banner; teaching good war to all citizen learners and future recruits; standardizing performance for increased profit and closing the poorest schools; and, in the United States, imposing the Pledge of Allegiance to integrate patriotic priesthood into teaching.

The three castes are better and more profitable for White men in teacher education, where male-dominated power structures prevail. While women represent the majority of teachers and of education students, in teacher education settings the old boys lead. Teachers colleges have tried to diversify their faculty by recruiting women and minorities. Although the number of women and minority professors has increased, nonetheless they are underrepresented (Chliwniak, 1997). Among the factors that contribute to this gap is that the societal concept of leadership rejects any alternative, feminist framework. The 'glass ceiling' and 'ivory tower' perceptions may be the result of a male-dominated organization. The academic workplace remains chilly and alienating for female professors and minority faculty, whose roles remain peripheral and often in conflict with institutional expectations. Women and minority professors also say that they are victims of salary inequities. The reward system seems biased so that they are perceived as less proficient than their White male colleagues, who often discredit feminist and minority concerns (Aguirre, 2000). There is often little in-depth consideration of the social forces that mould workplace socialization and professional satisfaction for women and minority professors; attention to these issues is limited and does not lead to organizational change. Where quality of working life and sex fairness should prevail, sex discrimination and stereotypes often dominate, perpetuating the traditional gender gap.

A feminist organizational approach could change these institutions. As organizational cultures affect curricula, a more inclusive style would ground the organizational values in community service. Such a change might contribute to eliminating collective behaviours that create a chilly climate for women and minorities. Should it be added that some of the worst enemies of feminism and recognition of the place of women seem to be women who adopt the male-dominant organizational views? To sum up, educational settings are urged to develop some consensus to combat the institutionalized norms of legitimacy and castes that exclude women and minorities. Deciphering and deconstructing the three castes of teacher education is but the first step towards building new models on a less discriminatory ground.

Sanctification, demystification: aren't these moves of the mind complementary aspects of a crucial educational process? A conceptual object is made so meaningful at a given time that it comes to be consecrated (Buchmann, 1992). In a second part of the same move, it is de-emphasized because it adumbrates other meaningful interpretations. Paradigmatic conceptions of truth and experience seem to express perspectives of discourse for which deconstruction proposes an analytics of difference. They are grids from which otherness is defined, to create the identifications that invite closures on meanings (McLaren, 1998). Dreams of liberation have mythic grounds.

A deconstructive reading of three prominent teacher education paradigms reveals problems encountered by each in satisfying its own theoretical postulates. First, the mastery learning paradigm promised experimental rigour at a time when this was valued among educational researchers. Yet an overview of the literature reveals that learning assessments rarely met the criteria of standardized testing, and control group designs inadequately tested educational objectives. Business is business, however; the advertisement made the idea sell. Second, the strategic teaching paradigm led to the decontextualized transfer of research on learning, and in the process became less sensitive to the contextualized nature of teachers' strategic thinking. But the war against mastery/ business provoked strategic breakthroughs. Finally, although the narrative inquiry paradigm upholds the importance of self-sufficient growth and autonomy, journal keeping is often enforced in a top-down authoritarian fashion and the expression of politically incorrect beliefs is discouraged. Narrative priesthood is indeed highly codified.

These three educational trends are reminiscent of the three stages that St-Julien L'Hospitalier, the hero of a story of Flaubert's (1876), must pass through. First he has to excel at hunting and perform in the countryside. Then he becomes a combatant, using strategy to win in battle. Only then does he reach the highest level of reflection, raising his thoughts to creation as a whole and merging with the divine. These phases undoubtedly match those through which our collective educational consciousness has passed. They represent a mythic taxonomy of human consciousness.

What about Reflective Practice Itself?

As an expression of theories about teacher thinking, the reflective approach has become a major, encompassing paradigm that brings together numerous ramifications. Ken Zeichner (1994, pp. 9–10) notes that 'It has come to the point now where the whole range of beliefs about teaching, learning, schooling, and the social order have become incorporated into the discourse about reflective practice. Everyone, no matter what his or her ideological orientation, has jumped on the bandwagon at this point and has committed his or her energies to furthering some version of reflective teaching practice.' Different trends in teacher education ascribe different specifics to the reflective approach: functional, strategic, personal, sociocritical, and so on.

The truth is that today all educational trends have become reflective. At present, all teacher educators appear to be committed to a secular priesthood. This fact raises new implications of the so-called evolution that has occurred. Within the practice of reflectivity there exist two diametrically opposed tendencies. One, which tends towards convergence, is narrative and constructive; the other, which tends towards divergence, is critically argumentative and entails deconstruction. In the first, narrative and constructive, tendency, which adopts a transpersonal orientation, teacher education may become a school for gurus. *Guru* is a word for teacher, but its explicit meaning is 'spiritual teacher,' the one whose knowledge of the truth brooks no appeal, the one who stands above. The guru transcends the crowd. Now, the highest level of reflectivity involves transpersonal values; indeed, 'pedagogy is typically individualized and holistic,' as observed by Zay and Day (1998, p. 4). The mere fact of setting the transpersonal as the goal of teacher education implies a taxonomy that situates some people above others. This transpersonally oriented taxonomy entails the same risks as the taxonomy of affective goals devised by David Krathwohl and his colleagues (Krathwohl, Bloom, & Masia, 1964). With this orientation, education could become indoctrination.

The risks involved in the second, critical and deconstructionist, tendency occur at the opposite pole. In the will to flatten all differences of status among individuals, exponents of the critical approach employ reflection in a dialectical deconstruction of all the principles that link people in obedience networks. This destroys the social web. Though it may seem hard to resist the ability to network meanings in one's own favour, the tenets of empowerment – the empowerment of otherness – lead logically to communities (so-called) of lonely, self-sufficient persons. There would seem to be not much to choose between academic subordination and reverence, and the loneliness of the fully grown-up student emancipated from all subordination, who resists becoming a master for dialectical reasons such as a code of ethics. All this in the name of teacher education. However, logic does not wholly control this human world.

Some people are reluctant to abandon the ideal of mastery, thinking, for example, 'What about the noblest aspirations of humankind?' or, 'What about all those years I spent attaining these bloody degrees?' The critical tendency has bequeathed a refusal of confidence in those who bear a message: being a messenger no longer gives messianic power that entails the surrender by others to the messenger's thinking. Belief networks have a direct connection with profitability. If nobody believes in anybody anymore, what about universities and teacher education? This is perhaps the reason most teacher educators seek the middle ground, that narrow ledge, as they work to shed light on the paradoxes of their own position.

It is at this juncture that I am inclined to denounce the other-worldliness of the view that truly reflective practice is a partnership, a partnership in which academics maintain the upper hand. For one thing, there are groups of practitioners who reflect very successfully without academics. For another, to talk of partnership is in reality to talk of the representation of interests that are inevitably divergent, indeed opposed. It would seem it is always difficult to create a partnership. Partnership entails clashes between institutions. A diluted version, in which, in order to elicit positive change and professional development, it is sufficient to guide one's partners in the field as they proceed through practical reflection, ignores the institutional aspect of this form of action. Cochran-Smith and Fries (2001) have demonstrated that many highly politicized debates about teacher professionalization aim at dismantling teacher training institutions and challenging their monopoly. Different ideological trends outside of teacher education institutions propose to deregulate teacher professionalization. Nonetheless what I try to demonstrate here is that *within* teacher education, regulation and standardization are ideals that are constantly challenged by practices. This is not to support rationales for placing certification outside the realm of the academy: there always will be needs for organizational settings where people can gather and reflect. I mean that change should be regulated from within and from the perspective that it can never be fully achieved.

For example, let's say that a system for relatively balanced joint action is designed by some external force to promote the process of practical reflection at several levels within an institution. Even in the best scenario, certain well-placed educators will take control of this empowerment system, stand above the melee, and channel the process in the direction that yields the best visibility for themselves. This could lead to a hardening of attitudes, designed to preserve gains, on the part of parties ill-prepared to enter into a phase of critique. Democratic processes would then lead to a reappropriation of leadership by representatives of various conflicting trends (practitioners, educators, academics, management), many of whom would find it easier to decry the inefficiency of the system for empowerment, and thus restore the status quo. One highly attractive pretext, for example, is to claim that those who designed the system wished to subordinate others to it. The most critical individuals would quietly set up their own order as though it emerged from the grassroots.

In situations like this, the opportunity arises to challenge these individuals' representation of events with quantified evaluations emerging from a large, representative sector of the population affected by the change. It then becomes evident that their sociocritical claims, while ill-founded, in fact work effectively in their own favour to undermine the initiatives taken, with no in-depth analysis of the true benefits and disadvantages of the proposed system for joint action. Support for manoeuvres of this kind may come from advisors – instructors or sociologists – making a show of neutrality, who, by revealing the risks of hegemony in the systems that have been put forward to elicit multilateral partnership, subtly make themselves indispensable. While persisting in a critical initial assessment, these advisors will not stick their necks out to propose an operational alternative solution.

Oh dearly cherished critique! Those who are the most vehement in their denunciation of the reflective practice instituted under the new approach, who were not given leadership in the initial process of change, will be adherents of other trends in reflective practice. They will prefer to scuttle the system of reflective practice in the name of reflective practice itself, by arguing that it doesn't tease out the highest levels of a reflective taxonomy (transcritical revolutionary thinking), working hard all the while to win others to their point of view. Finally, assuming that their own empowerment reaches peak fulfilment, they will most probably do everything possible to ensure their own system of reflective practice is secure and does not encounter the kinds of revolutions they themselves instigated against the previous one – both a proof and a reduction to the absurd of the notion that the previous system had reached the level of transcritical revolutionary thought, the level at which every educational method self-destructs.

The process would appear to be endless. If the taxonomy of developing reflectivity is ascending, there will always be people at the top ready to guide the insufficiently reflective at the bottom of the ladder. The logic of taxonomy is nomothetic, i.e., classificatory and comparative; it runs counter to the ideals proclaimed. Another current trend among many educators is to consider that reflection about oneself and one's own real-life cases has more educational impact than reflection on other people's cases. In reality, in workshops on reflective practice and other seminars for the analysis of practice, the contrary is often true. Here, a boundary is described between cases perceived as objects and cases that proceed from the subject. By adopting a subjectivizing position, the educator can cause the boundary to be transgressed and bring individuals to uncover emotions that underlie their practice, their representations, and their interpretation of situations (Blanchard-Laville & Fablet, 1998). Participants often find it easier to reflect in depth on cases that are not their own (not to mention fictional cases) because they feel less emotionally involved. They can voice their thoughts about themselves indirectly. In contrast, in workshops where the uncovering of the subject is an unalterable principle, we encounter strategies for covering and clothing feelings whose intensity appears proportional to the individual's sense that personal territory has been violated. Personal reality then becomes opaque.

And after all, who among us has no blind spots? Doesn't shining the spotlight on the other person's self entail entering into a power relationship with the meaning the other person ascribes to his or her own life, a relationship that could slip into abuse? Isn't the risk of abuse in working with another person's sense of self diminished if we engage in reflection on anonymous cases? In such circumstances, nothing prevents participants from linking personal events to the cases studied, bringing out those links that their own experience reveals to them. Then again, in this field there are no universal rules. Shared reflection is sometimes easier when the associated feelings are less intense. And in any case, the problem takes on a different aspect in the context of instructional approaches focused on knowledge and operating on disciplinary epistemology, in the context of instrumental approaches focused on interdisciplinary processes, and in the context of psychopedagogical or sociocentric approaches of a transdisciplinary kind.

Suddenly, thinking over the political parasitism that the verbalization of learning to teach represents, I experience doubt: Is our narrative action constituted exclusively of others' learning? Does our identity consist of transparency? I'm haunted by the spectre of social parasitism. While writing this I revisited a chapter by Smyth (1992 p. 300) that denounces his own activity as a writer; he proposes 'to jettison the oppressive view that people outside of classrooms know what is "best" about teaching.' Smyth emphasizes that 'people who do the work of teaching should be the same people who reflect upon it'; then he condemns 'deficiencies in teaching' caused by 'dominant groups in society [who] pursue their narrow sectional interests' (ibid). I argue with myself over the ambiguity of our role as the 'metateachers' we are. Certainly, the story we create concerning our role has an impact on our potential for social usefulness. We need to engage in a cleansing reflection on our own potential for reflective parasitism.

One implication of deconstruction is that no single paradigm is perfect and classroom reality lies ever beyond language games and the discourse of legitimation. Postparadigmatic analysis indicates, moreover, that even critical trends may be subject to critique. Then, what if motivation and enthusiasm now prevail where formerly mere survival was the rule? One moral might be that, if educators and researchers realize the relativity of their reciprocal legitimizing games, they may stop fighting and peacefully build their contradictions together in a patchwork of non-exclusive beliefs. And if professional enthusiasm, motivation, and relevance to action are the basic frameworks supporting theoretical efforts in teacher education, then it could be emphasized that proposals should preferably be grounded in moral purposes providing food for thought and dedicated action. A number of viewpoints could then be adopted by the same teacher in the course of the school year, as seems relevant. The eclecticism of lived teaching would become acceptable as a normal feature of practice. Not that teachers' rationality makes it difficult to handle 'pure' theoretical categories of action, but rather that theoretical models are by nature rationally limited to one viewpoint and only partly adequate for practical purposes. Like any good representation, theory should be explicit about important, valued facts; it should expose constraints on action in terms that make it easier to handle; it should be a coherent context to work in; it should be concise and abstract reality in an easy way; it should be understandable and scaffold processing in action; its execution should be feasible. Theory would then be considered representational and inductive, which is already a well-accepted, conservative notion. Above all, due to the representational nature of theory, the eclecticism of practice suggests that experienced practitioners could reach a level of competence where their frame of reference would be embodied in action. This frame would become self-sufficient and postparadigmatic: it would no longer express paradigmatic voices but individual and idiosyncratic realities.

CHAPTER TWO

Deconstructing Presence:
Behind the Educational Myth

Semiotic deconstruction should be understood as a positive use of criticism.[1] By locating the oppositions that organize value and power, it sheds light on their constructed backstage props. As educational models are also mental and social constructs, their critical understanding may seem to have a deconstructive, disillusioning effect, even though this effect has positive implications. Actually, deconstruction is instrumental in the reflective construction of meaning. As the critical arguments presented here take the form of an essay, they suggest in their own formalism that narratological postmodern criticism may reveal useful moral avenues to deconstruct some voice networks as being expressions of the self-authorized, narrative leadership of a few tenors and divas on an elitist stage. Also, because deconstruction is not meant to promote a network, it has to provide its own criticism.

Construction and deconstruction are complementary processes. For example, in the last few years the story maker has been emphasized as a major aspect of character construction. Story will not be complete if the place of the story maker is not clearly situated. When we talk about human characters, personal stories, and professional roles, story making builds new dimensions in a real-life time and space. It may cure, help, fulfil, and resolve; but it may also wreck the ship, cast all adrift, and dash hopes on the reefs. What is then beyond the narrative? Illusion or presence? Self or doctrine? Semiotic tools have been developed to analyse texts, and they apply to personal and social texts too. The narrative educational trend is a social text as well. Its deconstruction may help reveal its backstage: is narrative really constructive?

There certainly is an ambiguity in the title of the present chapter. Does *presence* represent a result of the deconstruction process? If so, who is backstage? Doesn't deconstruction demonstrate rather a reaction against the imposture of a presence behind the storied and restoried lives of teachers as expressed in their narratives? In effect, this ambiguity raises an issue with the stance taken in this chapter. As a story, narrative is past, and sometimes obsolete. It is never a present moment. Thus if there is a presence, it probably lies beyond what is captured by stories. The point here is not that present things are *not,* or do not exist; they certainly *are,* and their existence may be verified. While some narrative educators emphasize awakening and the realization of an inner presence, however, the role of presence in philosophy has long been a pretext for imposing absolute views in education. Suggesting presence, through or beyond individual story, has been an ideological argument for building indoctrination systems for centuries. How can this danger be avoided? As a way of destorying events, deconstructive criticisms may provide useful, political instruments that demystify the authority of narrative fundamentalists who claim that methodic awakening will be produced through an enlightening faith in the narrative tradition.

Thus deconstruction may provide a framework for narrative criticisms. But deconstruction should not become a goal in itself; it is not above its own deconstruction. If deconstruction must be, it can have no permanent presence by itself. It cannot then be assimilated with a method. Thus, so as to be meaningful, deconstruction should also be deconstructed when it has done its work; this metadeconstruction may free the idiosyncratic meaning from any attempt to legitimate an allegedly generalizable path to awakening. Metadeconstruction would provide criticisms of moral order.

This chapter will use the deconstruction framework to consider the following arguments:

1 The narrative approach in teacher education has not even begun to fully use the tools of narratology, even though this is one of its basic claims.
2 When transferred to teacher education, the narrative approach involves particular risks which must be acknowledged.
3 If the narrative approach consists in formalizing a new psychoanalytical path, it may then prevent more critical, social issues from emerging (Apple, 2000).
4 Self-awakening is by definition an individual, idiosyncratic experience that may not be generalizable in a narrative approach. Language differs from reality, culture from nature, and story making is

probably only partially concerned with the perception of truth and meaning.

5 By setting aside the psychological perspective, the narratologic critics might help deconstruct ideology, and thus approach individual autonomy with the least possible ideological imposition.

6 Deconstruction itself must be deconstructed in order to undermine its own ideological power.

This relativist approach denies the possibility of some metaphysical comfort. It implies that meaning is ever to be reconstructed, and does not reach a state of permanence.

Educational Narratology: What Philosophical Roots?

As usually expressed in the educational field, the narrative approach traces its most important sources to the post-Hegelian, Deweyan educational philosophy – thus pragmatism – in the biographic Chicago school, and in Polanyi's works on personal knowledge. Autobiography was certainly one of the first means used to study education, though it was temporarily rejected by behaviourists as being 'mentalist.' The experiential orientation of the narrative way of knowing makes it belong to the tradition of phenomenology and qualitative research trends. In the phenomenological analysis of human experience, a phenomenon comes into existence when it receives a name. Many aspects of the world are ignored by conscious awareness; they remain at the prephenomenological level of the ever-present continuum of uncaptured life, untransformed into experience. Experience then comes from the story humans make of it. For structuralists and 'I'-philosophers, experience has a past-future structure. Storying and restorying events make human experience existing, shared, and cultural. In this structural perspective, story allows victory over nature. In a post-structuralist perspective, however, story and nature are but signs.

Two opposite stances have historically been taken regarding prephenomenological perception. The first stance may be called idealistic, as it implies an epistemological sense of 'idea-reality first,' whether it be in the transcendentalist, 'I'-philosophy tradition of Descartes, Kant, and Husserl (subjective idealism) or in the immanentist, metaphysical tradition of Spinoza and Hegel (objective idealism). In the idealistic view, story is an object of awareness; there is a presence beyond the narrative, and ideas do precede language. Underlying this position is the hypothesis of a higher order of knowledge that may be reached and constructed as an experience-encompassing identity or wholeness.

This constructive, structural view contrasts with the postmodern view that human perceptions are cultural entities. Indeed, the second, post-structuralist stance turns the usual picture of the world upside-down. It defines language categories and social meanings as the ultimate reality. In that perspective, 'the priority of Culture over Nature now appears as a priority of the Sign over Objective Things, and the priority of Society over the Individual now appears as a priority of the Sign over Subjective Ideas' (Harland, 1987, p. 68). Although formalist (as were Plato's timeless forms), the philosophical predominance of the sign in post-structuralism should not be interpreted in materialistic terms, as would appear from the dualistic opposition idealism/materialism. In post-structuralism, the sign may express a meaningfulness which is neither idealistic nor materialistic, as will be explained below. The point of the foregoing considerations is to suggest that the narrative approach in education is inevitably integrated in some philosophical stance on the nature of signs and meanings. The perspective has deep implications for the way it is destined to contribute to education, to educational innovation, and to any supposed social or individual 'awakening,' if it does.

The narrative approach is not specific to educational sciences. Transposed into the educational world, narratives of experience indicate the way in which pupils and teachers, as well as researchers, story a life in constant motion, refining shared narratives supporting communities of thought. In this orientation, humans do not borrow their models from life but from the stories they collectively construct in transforming events into language. Humans acquire identity from and through discourse (Clandinin & Connelly, 1996).

Narrative inquiry may be *extradiscursive* (have an outward focus) when the viewpoint is external to the storied life: a teacher's biography may be reported by a colleague, an educator, or a researcher; it is then involved in a dialogic frame where the story is progressively deepened and linked through multiple indexations. But narrative inquiry may well be autobiographical. It is then *intradiscursive* (with an inward focus) and the teacher (or pupil, or researcher) keeps her/his journal, which corresponds to the self in a monological relationship: the narrative of experience is then close to the inner monologue, and the construction of meaning is internal. As will be seen in this section, narrative inquiry has not used all the possibilities of narratologic criticism. Also, its interpretive frame of reference is usually modern and structuralist, rather than postmodern and superstructuralist. In that sense, narrative inquiry has not fully developed its own contradictions (which may be enlightened by postmodern criticisms), nor has it yet exploited all its methodological tools. From a philosophical standpoint, narrative inquiry is most often framed in a traditionalist, idealistic perspective. On the one hand, it is story-centred and diachronic, historicist; on the other hand, it is moulded by Hegelian presumptions about an absolute truth underlying language and the structural construction of a state of permanence. This rigid assumption risks paralysis and schematism, as has been emphasized by postmodern literature. Be it extradiscursive or intradiscursive, the narrative inquiry is situated in a web of multifold goals. It cannot be systematically and entirely reconstructed in the ideal order and direction of some hypothetical presence-to-meaning, so that it can be easily reached by analytical tools. For that reason, semiotic tools always have limited textual purposes. They inhere in the language, whose meaning is always disseminated, and the way they provoke change may never be entirely circumscribed.

Data of narrative inquiry may be field notes of shared experiences, transcripts of semistructured interviews, stories of events, and case studies. Actually, they correspond to an ethnomethodological, practice-centred orientation of research. Research criteria are faithfulness to reality and the transferability of results. Again, in these methodological guard rails, the difference between events-as-reported and events-as-lived is emphasized in a dualistic way that reflects the above-mentioned contradiction between an idealistic, transcendent presence and a Wittgensteinian perspective on the embedment of language and facts. However, the narrative approach claims to be distinct from models of technical rationality. The contemporaneous phenomenological perspective adopted by ethnomethodology (since Garfinkel, 1967, and Schutz, 1967) would imply that the object of knowledge is not separate from the subject who is constructing its representation. On the theoretical level, this viewpoint differs radically from the metacognitive as well as from the idealistic perspectives, which are meant to target a transcendent knowledge of one's own knowledge. Rather, in the phenomenological perspective, meaning is in the context. This basic contrast seems to have been misunderstood by narrativists promoting awakening through self-story-making; which tends to indicate, in Derrida's words, that they have been overwhelmed by their own writing. A lack of coherence with their own philosophical roots may well have turned their story crusade into novelist aesthetics.

A close look at the claims of narrative inquirers indicates a few para-doxes. They claim an interpretive philosophy which is in the line of idealistic philosophers (examples are provided hereafter). This idealis-tic claim emphasizes the importance of awakening and an ultimate meaning, and supplies the framework of interpretation for stories of the personal. This first claim applies to the interpretive framework, that is, the way narrative meaning is justified. At the same time, a second, contrasting claim is made as to the way methodology is handled, i.e., in an experiential, contextualized, dialogical, and integrative way. Although this second claim does not fully contradict late Hegelian works and the metaphysical tradition of objective idealism, it integrates aspects of postmodernity such as contextualized and interactive meaning making. In other words, the method is claimed to be postmodern while the meaning to be reached through it is traditionally idealistic. Also, the defence of the narrative approach is its promotion of equality and sharing within communities, as a voice for the feeble and the oppressed; but the voice is raised by the powerful, who project guiding, irrefutable principles. At the present time, narrative inquiry is rooted in an ambigu-ous philosophical ground where idealistic tendencies and social mean-ing are confused. This contradictory, dual voice resembles any governing political discourse, where lie and truth merge in universal statements, where delusion and secrecy are common practice.

Educational Narratology: Which Semiotic Tools?

Earlier considered a simplistic form of literacy (Di Pardo, 1990), the narrative has returned to the international stage as a means of knowl-edge making in a mediated social discourse. The emphasis on the per-sonal aspect of knowledge making calls for a reconsideration of narrative, and a devaluing of depersonalized, dehistoricized essay forms. However, the narrative may at best become a personal and a social tool for reflect-ing situations, although it might prevent more critical actions from taking place. On the personal level, life story and its expression come to be linked to episodic features having a psychological 'depth' (Jung, 1964). Up to now, the narrative tools used for analysing personal stories and symbols have mostly been related to themes and metaphor analysis. Not much has been done to deal with specific organizational patterns of personal texts, like text markers, signal words, framing categories, and story grammars. In this section, I propose to deal with semiotic tools that might be integrated with the educational narrative inquiry, as they be-long to the realm of narratology.

Paul Ricoeur, in *Time and Narrative* (1984–8), analyses the relationship between existential time and narrative and studies the refiguration of temporal experience by narrative through the resources of an empirical inquiry aimed at detecting the influences of culture. Like Julia Kristeva in her work *Hannah Arendt: Life Is a Narrative* (2001), he makes a very strong claim for framing the experiential through narratives. As Hannah Arendt put it (quoted in Kristeva, 2001, p. 3), 'It seems as if certain persons are so exposed in their own lives (and only their lives, not as persons!), that they become, as it were, junction points and concrete objectifications of *life.*' Story-making processes configure life meaning, and reciprocally meaning reconfigures life narratives through the act of reading. Along this line of inquiry, Paul Perron (personal communication, 2001) emphasizes the role of narrative for the experiential and notes that the pedagogical situation reconfigures the narrative through the act of production and reception.

Ricoeur shows that the history of events has been eclipsed in French historiography. Neopositivist criticisms of narrative rejected it because centring on historical events 'shares the misleading assumptions of most common-sense notions' (1984–8, vol. 1, p. 96). The instruments of narrative inquiry mentioned in the educational literature indeed concentrate on events rather than on general aspects of classroom life. An inductive approach is used for analysing journal-keeping practices, interviews, and field notes. Note that these data collections do not usually arise from routine classroom practice and that they are mediated by or for the narrative inquirer. This approach provides a multilevel assessment and analysis on the basis of which a 'shared narrative unity' is negotiated (Connelly & Clandinin, 1990, p. 3). The scholarly technique for understanding narratives is usually a rough thematic analysis, on the basis of the researcher's active recording of how classroom events or teachers' conversations were constructed. The construction metaphor prevails, and, as pointed out above, without a critical deconstruction to parallel the discovery of patterns and structures, this discovery may become mere manipulation or just creation. Actually, the instruments of narrative inquiry seem very compatible with traditional content analysis techniques. Their claimed originality lies principally in their involvement of dialogue in the construction of meaning, and the mirror effect of feedback and reformulation. The focus on events is not specific to the narrative approach; the same orientation is found in ethnomethodology and cognitive research, in which the memory pointers are easier to activate when short-term events are in awareness or when episodic memory is activated. Some allusions to deixis (space and time components in discourse) lead the reader of narrative inquiry works to think that plot (time) and scenes (space), being very specific to narratology, have been used to construct the narrative meaning of and for the classroom, but this is rarely the case. Also, those tools have long pertained to cognitive science: segmentation of verbal protocols is made episodically where elements of time and space may be seized at the macrostructural level or at the microstructural, deictic level.

In the field of linguistics, the narrative approach does not fit into a definite typological textual framework. Educational narratology reports consistently mix argumentative and descriptive textual *genres,* and the teacher's narrative is merely embedded in a descriptive discourse that occasionally takes on performative, prescriptive functions. Textual, discursive approaches to narrative macrostructures are going far beyond what seems to be used presently in the educational analysis of classroom narratives, as far as methodological originality, rigour, and coherence are concerned, as well as the subject's experience and integrity (see, for example, Labov & Waletsky, 1967). Indeed, leaving the privacy of the subject untouched may denote tact, respect, and consideration. In contrast, it should perhaps be remembered that some narrative inquirers have assessment duties towards the subjects with whom they are said to chat nonhierarchically. From a critical perspective, the priority is a reciprocal, political awareness of influence processes, and finding 'ways of knowing that do not perpetuate power imbalances' (Lather, 1989, p. 14). But who can say for sure when participant observation is less authoritative than nonparticipative research?

Thus the present use of the narrative in teacher education does not owe much to narratology, even though this affiliation is clearly claimed. Instead, the interpretive aspects of personal stories predominate, and the psychological claim takes on a major role. For example, Clandinin (1991) introduced the concept of awakening through the narrative inner quest; the state of awakening is equated to a state of realization. Later in this chapter, I will emphasize the possible risks implied by a covert generalization of self-realization concepts. Here I suggest some of the benefits of keeping to a closer use of narratologic tools in the analysis of personal texts (Danesi, 1999b). Indeed, as a somewhat unsystematic model of thinking, the narrative approach in education does not really exploit the potential of narratology. Narratology is based upon the main research frameworks regularly used in literary analysis: story grammars, actantial analysis (analysis of the active functions in a story), narrative frame analysis, focal analysis (Eco, Santambrogio, &

Violi, 1988), and the semiotic square (Greimas & Courtés, 1989). I argue here that using these semiotic tools in case studies and in the approaches of personal and professional development might reduce the risks associated with the unreflected implementation of reflexive approaches and their psychologism. These semiotic tools are analysed hereafter from a teacher education point of view.

Story Grammars

As Ricoeur (1984–8, vol. 1, p. 178) puts it, 'The narrativists have successfully demonstrated that to narrate is already to explain.' However, in the field of teacher education one may wonder whether an increased awareness of narrative superstructures of experiential texts might not be a prerequisite of shared understanding. Hence the importance of story grammars. A grammar is a tool for analysing regularities in a text (the word *text* includes any verbal utterance that is seen or heard). A story grammar is a special case of textual grammar that analyses the superstructures of narrative texts. Story grammars are content-specific, intentionalized organizational patterns that refer to the syntactic, semantic, and pragmatic modelling of a story, as well as to the knowledge of that model that a person brings to bear. These analytical tools imply a knowledge of the types of regularities shaping narratives, and shed light on the textual and mental model of the narrative. A story grammar has three components (Van Dijk, 1973):

1 a *syntax* that specifies categories and their symbolic form, theoretical axioms, and rules for well-formed instances, instantiation, or transformation from axioms;
2 a *semantic* that defines possible interpretations of syntactic instantiations and relationships, and their abstract representations; and
3 a *pragmatic* that characterizes intentions related to the context of application of the grammar (how narrative discourse becomes functional and situated).

The grammar may distinguish the level of narrative performance and the level of narrative competence. Story grammars often use formal logic, and characterize predicate signs (relations and properties) and argument signs (individual objects). They involve primitive terms of the language, specific terms of the domain, building rules to specify correct sequences, transformation rules to define change and the dynamics of the story, a set of axioms or basic grammar rules that constitute the grammar and belong to the story system, and a set of technical symbols representing syntactic variables and constants. It may at first seem that such a rationale could not account for such aesthetic aspects of the story as metaphors. But symbols may also be used for representing unifying metaphors, basic metaphoric nodes constitutive of the narrative.

Also, basic aspects of story grammar are easy to use in a collaborative relationship. For example, Greimas's story grammar lays the necessary conditions for storying events, beginning with the least complex logical model possible. Actually, no story grammar has yet been developed to analyse life stories and case studies. But such an analysis might well represent a grounded approach to personal texts. Diverse forms of analytical grammar are used in literary analysis to illuminate superstructures and functions in a story, and may provide useful knowledge to narrative collaborative inquirers. They are possible ways of deepening the personal knowledge-making process of narrative inquiry.

Actantial Analysis

The actantial model makes it possible to analyse active semiotic components of the human imaginary. Stories may be decomposed into a sequence of narrative propositions, shedding light on functional narrative transformations. The actantial model was proposed by Greimas (1983) in the sixties, and is an abstract of Propp's (1928) folktale morphology. The *Subject* seeks the *Object* of her/his quest; she/he is helped, or opposed, by *Helpers* and *Opponents* that act directly on her/him. These actants may be abstract or natural forces (an opponent may be the wind or a lack of time). The *Sender* is the person (or feature, or event) responsible for initiating the quest; the *Receiver* is the actant for whose benefit the quest is undertaken. Actantial transformations are produced by syntagmatic (sequential) or by paradigmatic (associative) disjunctions of these actants. Two basic narrative propositions occur frequently: a Subject-Object relation $F(S \longrightarrow O)$ and a Sender-Object-Receiver relation $F(D1 \longrightarrow O \longrightarrow D2)$, where F defines the semiotic function. This simple grammar allows the analysis of narrative functions in a text, inasmuch as they constitute the active forces of a plot, around which subactants (helpers and opponents) interact. Thus the actantial model provides an analytical tool easily applicable to novels, narratives, personal stories, and myths. Its analytical structure may be mapped as in figure 2.1.

Figure 2.1
Greimas's analytical model of story actants

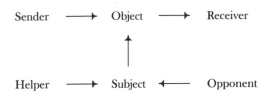

Actants in a story are like grammar functions: they constitute the basic organizers of events. The actantial analysis sheds light on the role of the active functions in the story, which may be humans as well as objects having a symbolic function. The six active functions may be used to analyse any human event: define who are the Subject, the purposive Object of the personal quest, and the Opponents (problems) and Helpers (aids) acting directly on the Subject in her/his quest for the Object. The Sender will be the thing or person causing the quest to begin, and the Receiver will be the thing, feature, or person to which/whom the Object of the personal quest is destined. According to Algirdas Greimas, many stories obey these basic narrative dynamics (note that in contemporary novels, some actants appear as anti-actants, such as anti-hero or anti-subject, when the Subject rejects its own attributes, and so on). For instance the Sender manipulates the Subject or Receiver, and theirs is a whole 'semiotics of manipulation different from (but linked to) a semiotics of action' (Greimas and Courtés, 1989, p. 577).

Actantial analysis might help practitioners frame their actions, purposes, and problems, without the presuppositions of a more psychoanalytical use of symbolism. For example, Michael, a middle school teacher, noticed that when he gave his classes, plans were never adhered to. He was still taking a lot of time to plan, but the more he did, the less it worked. Defining his situation in terms of active functions, he determined that his Object was planning, as demanded by the school (Sender) in the interest of pupils (Receivers). His Opponents were time and adaptation. His Helpers were his thematic projects, because they adapt to any classroom situation. Reflecting on the Object of his quest, however, Michael started to perceive that it was not well defined. Actually, his purpose was not really 'planning,' but pupils' work and motivation. Further reflection on his Opponents and Helpers led Michael to conceive a new way of planning whereby adaptive thematic projects helped

Figure 2.2
'Forcing a square peg into a round hole' (Sue)

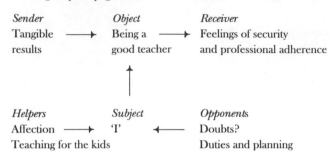

This basic story grammar traces the historical framework constituting the subject (Foucault, 1980). Meaning is not rigidly fixed, but becomes

accomplish his actual Object: lively work motivation in the classroom. Thus, this semiotic tool was useful for Michael as a means for problem solving. Now, here is the way Sue, a secondary teacher of French in Manitoba, reflects on a similar situation in her diary; her actantial analysis of the situation is in figure 2.2.

> My Achilles heel in teaching is long-term planning. I am already a very poor planner in general; I like to do whatever I feel like doing at whatever time I feel like doing it. To me, long-term planning is like wearing handcuffs: it subdues the beast and makes it controllable, but it is highly irritating. At best, I might plan for two or three consecutive classes, but beyond that, I am a dismal failure. A few times when I have undertaken sizeable projects, especially in Social Studies, I have been forced to write an outline of a plan. I know, and I've been told by many persons, that to plan for an extended period of time is a time-saver in the long run, but it doesn't seem worth it to me for the amount of time it takes initially. I'm happier taking things one day at a time, seeing how things go, trying this, trying that, rather than following a recipe, a plan! By the way, I hate schedules too, though they are extremely practical. I have never, in my life, been able to stick to a schedule for very long. By that, I don't mean being at work on time or meeting deadlines (give or take a day or two), but doing the same things at the same time, day after day, week after week. I am a free spirit, I need air and space, not handcuffs, chains, plans and schedules.

This basic story grammar traces the historical framework constituting the subject (Foucault, 1980). Meaning is not rigidly fixed, but becomes a site of departure for determining the social constraints shaping enunciative identities.

Narrative Frame Analysis

The importance of plots and scenes has been emphasized in the literature on educational narrative. The notion of *plot* is instrumental in story grammars. The plot links the actors, their actions, their goals and intentions, and circumstances inside one unity of time. The plot provides an organizational configuration that applies in a systematic sequence. This general narrative blueprint is prototypical and may be readily noticed during reading. There is generally an initial setting of narrative forces that is disturbed by an actant. The imbalance results in a quest, which ends when stability is recovered through the actions of major actants.

Many traditional narratives are built on basic movements such as Introduction – Trigger Event – Development – Transformation – Conclusion. Pointing out these dynamics of action as they occur in the classroom might bring a teacher a better understanding and control of these phases. For example, Irene noticed in her classroom that certain events were often the pretext for important positive or negative transformations in classroom relationships. She learned how to identify these plots and use them as pivots of positive transformations. Irene did so by grounding all further classroom activities in the key plots. Thus, this semiotic tool was useful for Irene as a basis for classroom decision making. A better understanding of classroom dynamics allowed her to direct transformations and effectively articulate conclusions as the introductions for new developments.

Focal Analysis

Whereas the *story* is a set of narrated events, the *narrative* is an oral or written discourse reporting these events. *Narration* is the fictive or real act producing this discourse, the telling act itself. The time and space of narration differs from the oral or written time and space represented in the *narrative*, which may itself enclose another time and space: those of the reported *story* (Genette, 1983). The story teller's viewpoint provides the focus of a narration. For example, the author may produce a fictive narrator in a time and place x telling the story of a time and place y. Thus the narrator (or story teller) may be a character in the novel. The narrator may also be said to be omniscient and provide information on past-future relationships among characters as well as on their private thoughts. These focuses are embedded in the narrative. Space/time focuses are the aspects of narrative that provide information about how an author situates him or herself towards his/her production. The analysis of focalization (or the viewpoint) reveals subtle intentions that implicitly support the partition of roles, of characters, which in turn influences the entire plot and description of scenes.

Focal analysis may apply to educational narrative too. The narrative utterance is a selection of constrained information in a set focus: meaning is expressed as long as situations authorize it. In the outward focus, the subject is submitted to external focuses and may lose control of her/his own role. In the inward focus, where the author is assimilated into a character, the narrator is gathering all perceptions, even those which concern him or her as an object. Here is an example, in Sue's diary, where the narrator is quite distinct from the author.

Dear Diary, let me introduce myself. I am Oscar, Sue's cat. Please don't be alarmed. Sue is fine ... I have simply gagged her and tied her to a chair. What could have motivated me to take such drastic measures? And why am I, her tabby cat, her devoted friend, writing in her diary? All shall be revealed, trust me. As a cat, I enjoy the privilege of going where I please, of eating and sleeping when I please and generally doing what I please when it pleases me. I also happen to please my mistress very much and she whispers all her secrets to me. I am usually very close-mouthed and an excellent keeper of secrets, but I had to break my silence. You see, enough is enough!

She happened to leave the last pages of her diary on a table for a few moments before tucking them into an envelope, so I had a rare opportunity. I've always been extremely curious (as cats are wont to be) about this diary and have asked her repeatedly to mention me in her entries. Well, those unattended pages were just too tempting, so I hopped up on the table and proceeded to read them. As you can imagine, this took a good deal of time and effort, and I had a great deal of trouble turning the pages. But it was certainly worth it. Don't believe a word of those last pages!

Sometimes I think I know my mistress better than she knows herself. I have always suspected this to be true, and now my suspicions are confirmed. How can she say that the traditional method of instructing children has not harmed her? Surely she was wearing her rose-colored glasses when she wrote that. I am here to set the record straight because I know what happened, I was there!

Focal analysis is basic to narratology and offers another way of shedding light on narrative regularities and uncovering a story's superstructures. The narrative focus reveals the place of the narrator in the story. The viewpoint may be particularly complex and subtle: the perspective of the narrator may appear in the deixis (expression of relationships to time and space) and in pragmatic modalities (expressions of doubt, anxiety, probability). Focal analysis may help in clarifying one's point of view as a living actor: is the point of view the one which was read or heard – in which case the subject is rooted in the social story (i.e., with an intranarrative viewpoint) – or does it come from a feeling of identity beyond the narrative, beyond the personal? For example, Michael, a teacher, had a tendency to model his thoughts on his readings, and his readings never kept to reality. At first he wanted reality to conform to his models, but he realized he was being shaped rather than shaping his own life. Analysing his focus made him aware that his life lay beyond the narrative. With his new extranarrative viewpoint, he stopped acting as if the story were imposed upon him and remaining just a character in the social play. He could see that, when being simply authentic in situations, he was bringing more energy to his pupils. Now Michael concentrates on authentic experiences rather than on the prescriptions of a book. As a semiotic tool, focal analysis was for Michael a step towards not needing tools anymore. He forged the path rather than being guided through it. Eventually, there was perhaps no path; he simply made his own decisions.

The Semiotic Square

The semiotic square is a logical tool that clarifies basic aspects of a story. This achronic tool sheds light on the conceptual orientations of a narrative by translating them into a spatial, relational frame of semantic contrasts. It works like a taxonomy, as a system defining four poles of mutual relationships. Dynamically speaking, the constituent relations of the taxonomic square are *regulated operations* through which meaning is produced or 'plotted.' Thus, a semiotic analysis of these constitutive relations illuminates transformation processes defined by the semantic poles and the syntactic operations among the poles. The four poles shown in figure 2.3 determine *knowledge positions* that frame story segments concerning either the action or the being of a character (Greimas & Courtés, 1989, p. 571). Figure 2.4 shows another way of expressing the same contrasts.

Figure 2.3
The basic semiotic square

True (being + appearing)
False (not being + not appearing)
Secret (being + not appearing)
Illusion or lie (not being + appearing)

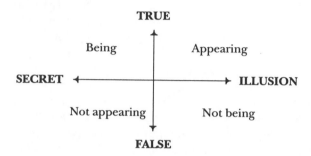

The categorical terms make it possible as well to determine states of being and characters in terms of their truthfulness (or *veridiction*). In a simple narrative, there is no distance between events and their knowledge. But knowledge of events may be dissimulated or disseminated in the narrative, and the level of truthfulness of events and characters has to be discovered by the reader. Knowledge of the degree of plausibility then becomes a *narrative pivot* for understanding the true coherence of the text (that is, its isotopy, the level of coherence binding meanings within the text).

Here I make use of an early Greimassian analysis of the paradigmatic dimension of narrative, as it can reveal some underlying textual features that represent useful text interpreters. The narrative interpretation could also take into account more recent work of an interactional nature that articulates the transformational, metamorphic dimension of narrative. Instead of a helper-subject-opponent ⟶ sender-object-receiver configuration, a methodology of inquiry could be founded on the more current interactional configuration of subject manipulating its anti-subjects, each endowed with its own distinct modalities of having-to, being-able-to, knowing, and wanting-to that are transformed as they interact with each other, which corresponds more to the actual classroom situation (as suggested by P. Perron, personal communication, May 2001).

Figure 2.4
A 2 × 2 translation of figure 2.3

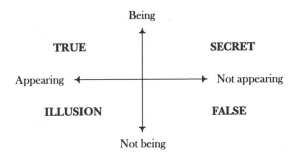

Figure 2.5
An application of the semiotic square to education, where ⟶ represents
implication and ⟷ contradiction

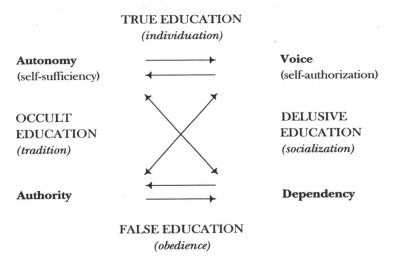

The basic assumption supporting the semiotic square is that any meaningful microuniverse may be analysed in terms of binary implications
and contrasts. Understanding these contrasts is useful for discovering
the underlying forces of a text, as well as of any socially constructed
meaning. For example, a teacher may spot relationships between educational action and the paradox of guided autonomy (figure 2.5). The

semiotic square analysis may help him or her understand that while personal voice may at best be the expression of individual actualization, it may also be the expression of adherence.

The conversion of figure 2.3 into figure 2.4, setting True/Secret/ Illusion/False into relations of contradiction and implication, is rather schematic. The same holds true for figure 2.5. A more nuanced discussion could also be proposed. Autonomy could be interpreted as the contrary of Dependency, and the way Authority is opposed to Voice may vary according to the situations, which is indicated by the crossed arrows in the middle of the figure. The emphasis here is on the use of this narrative superstructure as a guide to shared meaning-making processes, in video study groups for teacher education, for instance (Tochon, 1999a, 2001a).

Semiotic Tools: Limits of the Narrative Method

The narrative approach has brought about the idea that the creation of meaning is the purpose of story making, and that individual accomplishment is reflected in the stories people build around themselves. This might be true in some cases, but one might wonder whether life is lived in stories or whether story is not just a pretext for communication. The communicative aspect of stories has its value, but experience is probably wider than may be captured through story creation. A non-narrative type of meaning can be found beyond stories. Thus one might well take a stance opposed to narrative: story cannot capture the full value of time, of space, and of being and its dynamics; no word reaches the ultimate meaning; there is no path to it. Because speech separates mind and experience, separates the subject and the object, a narrative quest may increase the distance to this inner identity. At an extreme, by developing (say) conceptual submission to the collaborative interpretation of the narrative inquirer, the narrative approach might cause problems greater than those it was intended to solve.

Therefore the deconstruction perspective implies a revolution in the way we conceive methods. In a functional way, as perceived in post-modernity, methods should not implicate an ideological conformity. Rather, an eclectic plurality of methods is needed to expand meaning to idiosyncratic virtualities. Methods in postmodernity are considered epistemologically anarchistic (Feyerabend, 1975), that is, they help in finding truths other than those endorsed by the initial theory. Semiotic tools are relative and do not represent an absolute; they leave the individual free to follow her/his own path.

In a short time, narrative has become another educational habit and a conformity network. Semiotic tools are proposed here for deconstructing such conceptual habits. Semiotic analysis might be used for discovering meaning and unravelling the network of ideological conformism underlying educational stories. Personal deconstruction sheds light on implicit superstructures of meaning, and may be socially critical. These analytical tools should not be taken as goals in themselves, however. Their purpose is to be meaningful, but they have no pretension of transmitting a state of inner presence. Semiotic tools of narratology do not necessarily imply a psychological approach to the person or the help of someone else.

These limits must be mentioned because, in educational practice, a series of contradictions arise. Some libertarian educators impose a journal-keeping practice whose stated purpose is to help teachers realize their autonomy; these teachers may immediately cease to attend their education classes and their educator has no choice but to administratively accredit their unexpected self-sufficiency. At another educational site, researchers guarantee anonymity to the studied teachers, so as to favour confidence and fulfilment through writing, but the teachers want to be considered co-authors of the papers in which they participate. One 'autobiographied' teacher became the target of intimidation by her colleagues, who disapproved of her star-image after her narrative case-study became a best-seller. In preservice education, student teachers now spend their white nights filling a compulsory diary rather than listing objectives. In classes, the traditional 'tell me about your last vacation' has become 'keep your personal journal.' Third-grade students keep a journal. Fourth-, fifth-, and sixth-grade kids have journal-keeping practice too. What is written in middle school? Answer: A diary. In so many high schools, every day starts, after the prayer or the national anthem, with 'Dear Diary.' In social education, in teacher education, everyone spends hours keeping an exhaustive, exhausting diary. Researchers suddenly realize that journals they analyse are both empty and wordy, full of empty words: thinking is quasi-absent, class contents are simply rehashed. As Sue noted in her diary, 'You see, I've come to realize that much of what I've been telling you is simply factual, not really analytical or reflective. I don't think you want a synopsis of the week's events. I shall try to go one step further, or deeper, as the case may be.'

The intensity of professional activities is such that few have time for deep thinking. At this time of uncertainty, some meta-educators have latched on to narrative inquiry and promote the new wave: guiding the faithful to awakening. Does the quest for autonomy make it necessary to obey their principles, touted as a universally applicable method? With no narrative education, is there no awakening? The bottom-up innovative process would then, by a subtle shift, be manipulated from above. The procedural dynamics of change would be frozen in a dogmatic body of declarative do's and don'ts. These details are not unimportant to the central argument of the present essay, but raise the curtain on the hidden backstage of some new trends in narrative education.

Even as educators promoting autobiographical narratives have acknowledged the importance of autonomy in the knowledge-building process, they have actually formalized this autonomy into a method. As soon as the method is generalized in teacher education, the generalization principle infringes on individuation processes. In the case of narrative autobiography, this educational model is contradicted by its aim: stimulating autonomous awakening and self-liberation. Thus, the narrative approach might be invalidated through the arguments which served for its validation. Indeed, educational autobiography may at worst lead the violation of subjects' personalities, to a penchant for transpositions of reality characterized by distancing from oneself for the purpose of passive self-observation. Or it may well be instrumental in imposing coercive methods, thereby handicapping the alternative, differentiated paths suitable for some individuals. The narrative approach may cause teachers to become submissive to a particular educator, who may tell them how to think, and articulate the criteria for good thinking and their own awakening as if those were generalizable. My stance is not that methods can or should be avoided. It is that methods are limiting by nature, and their use in a mediated so-called self-actualization may only be delusive (see table 2.1).

It touches on the very peculiar relationship that evolves between a journal-writer and a journal-reader. The more a person reveals her/himself in her/his writings, the more vulnerable s/he becomes emotionally and morally. When you let another person into your journal, you are letting them into [your] head. What are the consequences? What is the price? For that reason, do you not think many if not all 'forced' journal writing will be half-truths? Will reflect the writer's image rather than a true, objective image? I suggest that no matter how 'truthful' and 'accurate' one may claim (or wish) to be in one's autobiographical, confessional writings, these will always be, to a great extent, a creative work of fiction. If this is the case, then whom is the educator really speaking to? To the writer's representation of

Table 2.1
The uses of personal narrative

Its possibilities	And its risks
Developing personal knowledge	Enhancing the role of teacher educators as moral scaffolders
Theorizing practice	
Linking professionalism to experience	Psychologizing and psychoanalysing development
Connecting personal history and profes-sional attitudes	
	Becoming dependent
Generating dialogue	Uncritically adopting implicit ideological norms
Improving listening	
Introducing the historical dimension in terms of identity on both individual and community levels	Submitting oneself to conformity, a network, or a guide
	Pathologizing professional problems
Increasing the coherence of one's system of thought	Developing verbal rather than true identity
Improving mental balance	Developing egotism and/or delusory experiences
Giving rise to better self-perception	
Sharing experiences and building on common knowledge	Imposing institutionalized confessions
	Mistaking narrative tools for life goals
Finding life goals	Justifying inaction
Suggesting action	Justifying gossip as a type of criterial evaluation
Promoting writing	

her/himself, then. Is that important to know? As a journal-writer, I can, at any moment, change my person, speak with forked tongue, if I wish to do so, in the interest of self-defense. Who in their right mind wants to be penetrated against their will, raped if you will? Besides, how true can your aim be if I keep moving the target? (Sue's metacritical diary)

Of course, authors of narrative inquiry have argued about the risks, dangers, and abuses of narrative and its 'two-edged inquiry sword' (Connelly & Clandinin, 1990, p. 10). The goodness in storytelling is a point of concern. But a deeper concern is related to the essential nature of narrative inquiry itself. As expressed in the teacher education litera-ture, narrative inquiry is meant to 'probe into the participants' past and future,' to penetrate deeply into 'experiences, to trace the emotionality attached to her/his particular way of storying events,' and by doing so, enter an affective community of thought to analyse with an educator the 'ongoing experiential text' (Clandinin & Connelly, 1989a, respectively pp. 11, 12, and 10). The educational experience is described as a means to reach a *universal meaning* (p. 3); the narrative quest is then elevated to religious experience (in William James's terms). Elsewhere it inhabits the couch of psychoanalysis, working on verbal imagery and embodied image, 'gathering up experiential threads meaningfully connected to the present' (Clandinin & Connelly, 1989b, p. 4). Narrative inquiry, as it is usually known in teacher education, focuses on individual psychology and may become *narrative therapy.*

Fundamentalists of educational narrative offer a psychic, inner revelation, a traditional sanctity providing basic methods for personal and social growth. This fundamentalist perspective may be historically explained by looking at the idealistic roots of pragmatism. Pragmatism developed a joint perspective of moral (e.g., religious) development and functional action in a unitive, practical, and goal-directed phenomenology. Also, William James (as well as Peirce) had been initiated into Vedanta. Vedantic monism places the unity of consciousness in the perspective of an all-pervading, absolute reality. The 'enlightened eye' of Eisner's (1991) qualitative researcher, 'authenticity,' and 'awakening' seem to belong to the same idealistic tradition. In this tradition, the growth of the self arises from master-disciple relationships and dialogue in a community of thought sharing a common ideology. We may find traces of this tradition in papers advocating growth towards personal unity: 'Unity means the union in a particular person in a particular time and place of all that he has been and undergone and of the tradition which helped shape him ' (Clandinin & Connelly, 1989a, p. 4). From this point of view, education would be an initiation to *presence.* Philosophically speaking, it may seem at first sight difficult to understand how this vertical, traditional relationship can fit in with a horizontal, nonhierarchical collaborative inquiry.

Now, linking the experiential, meaning threads to this awakening appears even more problematic. Who does it and by what means? Is the unifying factor the community's discourse, tradition, or the individual voice? The 'tradition against the Logic of reduction' (Clandinin & Connelly, 1989a, p. 7) may reveal itself more reductionist and interventionist than it claims to be. Unstructured interviewing and a researcher's experience-sharing implies stepping outside the usual boundaries in an interview setting. Whereas good semistructured interviewers are those who speak the least, the narrative inquirer may be very involved in the conversation and may then interfere in the process in an implicit, normative way. For example, some narrative inquirers express personal concerns about what the interviewee said, and about death and survival. The advantages to that position lie in empathy, for example, but there is also a clear danger of manipulating and indoctrinating the interviewee. Adopting objective ways of collecting data has been declared sinful by the devotees of narrative. But the sin of objectivity may be preferable to exercising a researcher's subjective influence on the individual's emotions, methodically invading privacy and encroaching upon the subject's identity.

Personal analysis of another is the domain of the psychologist and the physician. It is not certain that clear cautions have been issued to avoid the well-known risks of countertransference, projection, and identification so common in these interactions. Psychoanalysts usually have coaching sessions among peers to clear out shifts in the analytical process. Narrative inquirers may not be well-enough equipped to face cathartic awakenings. Also, the specificity of the pedagogical intervention may be replaced by a grand orientation, keeping the real problem of the teacher's self-sufficiency out of sight.

Postmodern Relativism: An Anti-Story

Up to this point, it has been argued that a self-constructionist perspective in education may lead to dogmatism and indoctrination, in the tradition of idealistic 'I'-philosophers. This becomes a major risk when methodic psychological tools are developed to make privacy public and to share a guided awakening. In contrast, let us analyse what a postmodern orientation could offer in the quest for reality. The arrival of post-structuralism was marked by Derrida's works on grammatology, speech phenomena, and writing difference (1978). The post-structuralist theory of language is built upon the reversal of Husserl's phenomenology of language. In effect, Husserl considers truth as being an expression willingly lexicalized by utterers. Meaning, in Husserl's theory of language, is conscious and intentional; it implies individual voice. Truth is then intrasubjective and monologic. To this stance, Derrida opposes the dialogical reality of an intersubjective space in which meaning is created through relationships rather than through the revelations of an inner time and inner voice. In Husserl's terms, the inward voice is adjacent to awareness; the seat of knowledge is already shared before being formulated into words. This viewpoint proper to 'I'-philosophers is questioned by the sociocritical trends whose key figures are Derrida, Gadamer, Habermas (though anti-pragmatist), and Rorty.

In contrast with the unsubstantial presence of an inner self, Derrida makes an absolute of writing. Writing is a space where dialogue becomes atemporal and intention becomes self-sufficient, whether the utterer is absent or even dead. For Derrida, writing has priority over other types of language, such as speech; writing is the true level of language. The written sign is always received rather than sent, and the writer is reader, an interpreter of the written sign which then belongs to a culture. In that way, Derrida does not treat written signs like natural signs, and for him meaning is not located in any one mind. In Derrida's view, beyond language there is only absence and emptiness, and the signified is merely an illusion, for it does not exist. The signifiers themselves are signifying, or pointing to, other cultural traces. Meaning is then produced by signifiers in motion, with infinite, unstoppable implications. Thus, meaning is never fully reached, because it is disseminated in language. Through dissemination, the sign's real being reveals itself as an anarchical and unpredictable subversion beyond either the writer's intentions or social control. Language is entropic, in an everlasting, unbalancing movement. Also, there is for Derrida no third term between Nothing and Being (i.e., in Kantian and Hegelian terms, no Becoming), because motion is mechanical. A mechanical motion cannot comprehend, and does not rise up in a synthesizing concept or an absolute idea. In this way Sue defines her becoming in the tension between nothingness and being: 'Almost every day, I ask myself, "Do I like teaching?" The reply varies from a definite NO to an uncommitted YES to an unconditional ABSOLUTELY. This all happens in a not quite conscious nor unconscious way (perhaps "mechanical" is the best way to describe it). It is *my* evaluation, on a daily basis. It is the only question that really matters, to my mind. One thing is for sure; if I loved teaching as much as I love writing, the profession could claim to own my soul. But such is not the case, nor will it ever be. But one has to earn a living, right?' (Sue's diary).

In the postmodern concept, the world is language. Writing creates the categories of the world; it is grounded in arch-signs which act as causal forces. The world itself is always a representation. Moments of now are perceived after they happen, and the present is always perceived as past. The absolute present is deconstructed as an illusion; the atemporal dream of the present moment is apprehended only in terms of aftereffects. Matter becomes meaningful through configurations of differences that appear when their shape has been deconstructed by reflection. Thus, in reflection, patterns of formal difference may merge in a signifying meaning which has infinite and universal implications. This unfolding meaningfulness spreads out void; emptiness appears as an antidote to the self-oriented, goal-directed story of life. It is the end of the story. Nothing would precede signifying. This post-structuralist stance is claimed above rationality and scientificity.

Deconstruction is understanding the impossibility of getting it right. It is not a method. Rather it appears to be a kind of situated wisdom. Deconstruction is a critical strategy implying radical transformations in the interrelations between knowledge and language. It does not rely upon an absolute truth. Rather, it is meant to unravel the power and authority at work in meaning and interpretation. Deconstruction is politically active: it is intended to change the signifying process, to destroy the *fabula* or scenario of the expressed narrative, and expand its lack of significance and its relativity to ultimate implications. One ultimate implication is emptiness, at once beyond story and fully integrated into the story. There is no absolute in the story nor in story making; action takes precedence. There are just interpretive processes, slips and slides of meaning. Just language in motion. Thus narrative creates the delusion of manipulable knowledge and meaning, and it may prevent the individual from finding his/her own ultimate implication. Context and story undergo radical transformations through deconstructive criticisms. Deconstruction is not problem solving. With deconstruction there is neither an Absolute nor a path to some sort of awakening. There is no coach but the signs and interpretations. Knowledge is not at issue in the deconstructive process.

Metadeconstruction: An Ethical Criticism

People who work on Derrida's narratologic theory usually notice its similarity to some aspects of Buddhist philosophy. In Madhyamika philosophy, there is a story about two opposed schools of thought. The first, nihilist school said, 'There is *nothing*.' But the second school remarked, 'Did you notice there *is* nothing?' There had to be an *awareness* of nothing. The Madhyamika, Middle Path school does not definitely espouse one of these two views. It is said reality just *is*, but there is nobody to check (Trungpa, 1973).

This seems a wise position to take concerning the possibility of presence beyond the narrative. Any definite claim may mislead the seeker. And the circularity of words may delude, on the path to any ultimate meaning that may exist. (Not to say that there is no meaning, but a more mindful position might avoid giving names to the unknown.) As educators, do we have the right to fix a definite path as the one and best way? Is this correct in any case? Some questions should perhaps be left as such because no words can answer them.

However, there is a risk in deconstruction itself (see the afterword in Bruner, 1986). Pragmatically speaking, in order for meaning to be functional it must be not only aesthetical, but ethical. The purposefulness of meaning necessitates a moral stance. This moral stance might be the critical one, in that a postmodern criticism denounces arbitrary power relationships. Meaningful power would become an ethic of action, respectful of individual differences. Not unrelated to the foregoing hypothesis about the sort of power that is socially meaningful is the evidence, in the recent literature on innovation, that personal transformation in a teacher cannot be imposed by academic authority or ideological sharing communities. A recent trend of innovation consists in planning implementations in the name of bottom-up, spontaneous field change; part of their promoters' work is to make the field people forget that this idealistic concept is a top-down percolation. In contrast, deconstructing the top-down process would help dispel illusions and thwart disinformation.

But isn't deconstruction, inasmuch as it instigates the end of the story, a paradoxical vacuum-cleaning anti-system, implying idiosyncrasy beyond any type of generalization? Then the deconstruction might nevertheless implicate a third element, a Kantian cue, an individual virtuality in the absence of permanence, something neither transcendent nor immanent, at the junction of cultural writing and reading, of teaching and learning. It may suggest an underlying transformational process towards meaningfulness. In the push for a renewed pragmatism, one might then propose an ethical deconstruction using semiotic tools for reconstructing the possibility of an education free of dogma, respectful of individual differences.

> But what is wrong with teaching? For one thing, there are a lot of Politics in teaching, in the school system ... In order for one person to get what they want, students' best interest is not always served. Is it in the best interest of the students to cause their teacher grief by giving her an inhumane workload? Is it in the students' best interest to allow an angry, disruptive child to torture the teacher day after day (kicking her desk, constantly whining about assignments)? Is it in the students' best interest to encourage them to think highly of themselves (self-esteem) and be content with themselves at the expense of discipline, self-discipline, good manners, and plain old respect for others?? Is it in the students' best interest to label a child as 'special' and let her get away with unacceptable behavior, such as leaving

the classroom when 'things get too tough' or 'she's feeling bad'? Is it in students' best interest for their parents to begrudge us our salaries and our vacations? Well, my tirade is spent, and Dear Diary, I say 'arrivederci.' (Sue's diary)

The importance of a critical approach to education has been emphasized throughout this chapter. Psychologism and neoromantic idealism tend to transform the use of personal story into a freelance psychoanalytic path. The potential risks of this path were suggested here: conceptual submission, thinking through a conformity system subtly imposed through language, loss of individuality. The narrative system of thought may justify a lack of responsibility towards action. On that point, biography is perhaps more realistic than the narrative approach, and its ideological implications are fewer. Biography places action on a chronological line which may stimulate a self-evaluation; the balance is then directed towards action.

Questions have been asked here from the perspective of knowledge rather than of affect. I do not mean that love, care, and affection should not exist in an educational process. The everyday experience of numerous educators confirms the existence of precious moments when communication is uplifted. I do mean, however, that love, care, and affection do not obey catchphrases and guidelines. Systems based on such catchphrases and guidelines have most of the time been translated into coercive evaluations and observation grids. Because present education is a mass system, such catchphrases and guidelines represent a danger for individual freedom and difference. Everyone has her/his way of expressing higher-level values.

In the direction of love, care, and affection, sharing narratives of experience is certainly progress, because it may enrich individual relationships. But the problem arises when so many people adopt narrative as a way of thinking. The tool becomes the goal, and the initial intention seems lost. Cliques are formed, and the approach is fixed in a doctrine. This is the reason I have emphasized deconstruction here as a useful complementary process. An idealistic stance should not be adopted without clear knowledge of its implications, maintaining criticism as a safeguard.

This chapter has suggested the need to examine in detail the nature of voices triggering veridical assent in the narrative community. In sum, I have outlined the junction of a critical perspective and the emerging educational narratology. Also, I have suggested a path for conducting research with the complementary use of constructive and deconstructive aspects of knowledge. Critical resistance should be applied to the discourse of liberation and narrative awakening, as such directions imply a basic ambiguity: the language of freedom is used for building obedience networks (Pinar, Reynolds, Slattery, & Taubman, 1995). In that domain, investigations should be carried out with some degree of independence from what semioticians have called 'the narrative ghost in the discursive machine' (Maddox, 1989, p. 675): 'The best way to cope with a world in which rivalry among the voices of veridiction is part of the normal course of things is neither with solipsism nor silence but by active cultivation of the critical competence to discriminate ... Toward that end, semiotics can prove to be a valuable help, but only by acknowledging that, on a planet which, thanks to accelerating communication, is constantly shrinking like Balzac's *peau de chagrin* and is always destabilized by the discourses of mankind, theory must turn its attention from exclusive emphasis on retrospective classification of meaning effects to prospective calculation of the effects of meaning.'

CHAPTER THREE

The Situated Researcher and the Myth of Lived Experience

The first and second chapters of this book dealt with the deconstruction of crucial aspects of myths that model teaching and teacher education: the myth of standard productivity, of a strategic fight against ignorance, and of the priestly role of educators who lead school change with such idealistic words that they make easy targets for people outside of education arguing for accountability. The argument for measurable results is often used to dismantle education as a democratic institution and open it to the marketplace. We tend to think and argue through myths, and there is nothing wrong with this. However, the link to practice is currently being re-emphasized in teacher education, as this is the place for improvements. We have to demonstrate that a democratic dialogue among teachers and schools of education can bring deeper and sounder results than the teach-to-test trends advocated by politicians. In this light research must be more situated.[1]

I coined the term *situated research* in 1993 while studying interactions in bilingual Manitoban settings (Tochon, 1999b). Situated research locates the researcher as a person conversing with educational situations, teachers, and students, to help them construct meaning and action. Rather than hiding the personal, psychological background of the researcher, situated research includes it as a component of its conversations with practice (Zeni, 2001). Integrating issues of gender, race, and social class, situated research acknowledges preconceptions, raises sociopolitical consciousness, and brings values to teaching (Ladson-Billings, 2001). It gives expression to all the roles of a teacher in school life: magician and artist, patrolman and waiter, pedagogue and critical spirit (Barone, 2001). Its aim is not to construct a new scientific mythos but rather to help other teacher-researchers and educators reflect on their own experiences to improve their action through a grounded philoso-phy. It is an emerging and shared symbolism rather than an imposed set of symbolic rules.

Situated research rests upon the analysis of narrative schemes, links, and spun metaphors in the events of personal life and observations. This process, understood as the recognition of contextual links after the reading of life events, has been named *post-structural recognition*. The analytical process involves a linking of the researcher's life knowledge with current events; the two intertwine in the narrative scheme of a diary report. The report exemplifies an inner and outer slice of life that are part of the life story of the situated researcher. The aim is to enter a conversation with others; the same effort at finding recognitional post-structures is asked of the reader. The researcher does not impose a definitive interpretation on the natural movement of contextual links.

For the purpose of passing on knowledge of life, theoretical and mathematical reductions of life are less practically resilient and sturdy than narrative accounts. Situated research is transformative. In making its point, therefore, the present chapter provides neither figures nor theoretical codification. In this chapter, I submit to the public some entries from a journal I kept to accompany a research project. My goal is to shed light on the delicate relationship between life story and situated narrative. The subject will be handled via experience clothed in the flesh of daily life.

In classic terms, 'life story,' as it emerges from the work of the Chicago school and from ethnomethodology, is differentiated from the narrative approach that developed later. The life story focuses on duration; the researcher participates very little. The researcher allows the interviewee to rearrange his or her own constructs and refrains wholly from inter-pretation (Seidman, 1991), or else reports on recurring features in order to identify quasi-social trends of thought. In a life story, the point of view tends to the sociocritical; situated research has a more personal viewpoint. The latter approach entails a participatory conversation with the interviewee.

I should like nevertheless to examine certain aspects of these topics that often go unmentioned in the literature. In particular, I consider the distinction between the private and the public spheres to be important because it brings to light certain processes of identity transformation. Whereas the life story retains a certain element of objectivity, situated narratives enter unreservedly into a new model, in which reality is seen as socially constructed. Situated research centres on shared subjective interpretation; with this approach, the constructed nature of interpretation emerges as more significant than the verification of recurring features. Clearly, each approach has advantages and drawbacks. The limits of the narrative approach have been emphasized in earlier works and in chapter 2 (Smyth, 1992; Tochon, 1994).

The distance between the territories occupied by these two approaches has been growing ever narrower, however; and at the frontier itself, two ways of viewing reality, that is, two epistemologies, are differentiated. The issue overlaps Hayden White's (1978) demonstration of the distinction between fiction and factual representation. The simple fact of making a life story public means formalizing the conceptual connections among the experiences reported. By certain processes of abstraction, facts that have been processed into memory are clustered round a few kernel metaphors, metaphors that are convincing enough to compel the listener's or reader's attention. This point is demonstrated below.

Since my aim is to recount through experience, I shall refrain from any analytic commentary on the entries quoted below from my research journal. I leave it to the reader to undertake reflection.

Winnipeg, 3 May 1993

I've just finished observing a class this morning. My aim was to get the teacher to talk, following the observation, about how her lesson planning and the adjustments made to the lesson planning during class are tied in with a personal and social life story. This was the third period of the morning; the teacher had already taught two tiring classes where she'd been forced to shout and assign several punishments. In third period she knew she could relax a bit. This was 'private journal' time. With a mechanical air, the pupils took down their notebooks, which were perched at the very top of a cupboard, away from prying looks. Once the notebooks had been distributed, they went to work writing, seated in all kinds of positions. The class was quiet for thirty long minutes.

After class, the teacher told me how restful this particular classroom activity is for her. In fact, she finds it restful to keep her own journal when she has the time. Right now I'm delighting in meta-rest, reflecting on how this teacher rests while writing entries in her journal about the way the children behaved while writing entries in their journals. Journals have become the opium of the classes. And I wondered, while talking to the teacher, if as an educator I choose journal-writing as a way of getting a rest from my student-teachers. The appeal of the written scream is that it is rarely disruptive. Quite probably, translating one's voice into jour-nal-keeping practice is not very disturbing because one is not truly honest. When teenagers start getting really honest in their journals, they're told they're not respecting classroom rules. Essentially, they are being asked to produce a fiction about themselves, though it's true that this institutionalized confessional sometimes reveals cases of abuse (the way the education of the young under Hitler did, but the definition of abuse was different then). So even a private journal, once institutional-ized, is subject to rules of compliance. Making it public means forcing it to embrace social goals. The extreme example of the private journals used in Mao's rehabilitation camps during the Chinese revolution testi-fies to this phenomenon. Once a journal has become a public event, it enters into the political. Going public seems to produce a distortion of the personal by subjecting it to ends beyond itself.

An interview with Alain Tanner, the Swiss filmmaker, comes to mind; I saw the interview on TV two days ago. Tanner's latest film shocks by presenting a woman's intimate diary uncensored. Tanner didn't censor his shots either, in particular one where the heroine decides to shave her pubic hair. The actress was interviewed following the interview with Tanner. She told how she played a major part in the film's production. It was she who determined the scenario (her own diary) and the shots. The filmmaker gave the actress a voice and she took possession of the screen. Yet at the moment of filming the difficult scene, she felt she was being gazed at. She felt she was watched rather than heard. The scene repre-sented such a difficult choice that afterwards she got out a bottle of wine – she never drinks.

I am of Swiss origin. Tanner's demonstration, and the paradox of liberation that imprisons, absorb me. Liberty that one person lays claim to within the shelter of legitimacy provided by another can become a straitjacket. The Swiss are capable of being prudish and fearful, having been overprotected, perhaps, by comfort. People like Ursula Andress have really not changed this mentality much. Yet in some Swiss artists I find an avant-garde approach that astonishes me. For instance, Tanner's film addresses up-to-the-minute controversies such as the acknowledgment of otherness, culture shock, unveiling, the empowerment of women, the actor's intervention as author.

The actress's gesture under Tanner's signature broaches a universe of signs where at one and the same time it will both find its own logic and be robbed of originality. So long as an idea is new, the accompanying new conceptual development surprises. In a narrative, the unfolding of the plot implies a metamorphosis of the initial situation. But when an idea has become part of our mores, it goes unnoticed. Pubic hair coiffeurs open up shop in San Francisco, the logic of unveiling corresponds to a fashion trend. Since Roland Barthes (1967), this logic has been seen to be in dialectical relation with its inverse, that of covering-over ... because the erotic is a matter of the covered being unveiled and of nudity being hinted at – a principle that post-Barthesian intellectuals of the fashion world have in fact applied. By analogy, these principles apply equally to the other type of unveiling, the publicizing of personal matters.

I sometimes wonder how it's possible for vast numbers of people to get caught up in debates over fashion and sexuality when one-third of the world's people are going hungry and another third are struggling with grave illnesses or shortage of money. My thoughts about life transformed as narrative are not merely playful. I am reflecting on the way something that, for anyone who's ever strolled on a European beach in summer, is a commonplace matter, undergoes cross-dressing, dressing-up, reconstruction, and ultimately unveils the person. The parallel that can be drawn with the way an author may transform her or his life story into narrative seems to me very revealing. An experience that was lived in all its nakedness is clothed with the concepts best suited to conveying how it looks when stripped bare.

The erotic dimension of a narrative of the intimate seems to hang on the intelligent arrangement of unveiling and covering-over. Does this erotic dimension correspond to the life story? Or does the narrative dress up experience with accessories that enhance its nakedness? Examining the pleasures of the text, Barthes (1973) articulated the erotics of writing as the unveiling/covering-over of the self. In the same vein, when Paul Ricoeur (1990) conceives of the self as an other, little conceptual innovation is involved, for he is writing in a tradition similar to that of certain existentialist reflections. He could even be reproached with using a phenomenological veil to cover over the alienation that may be entailed in coming at the self through the inspiration of the other. The narrative liberation of the self can alienate: Socrates never wrote.

Nowadays, fashion shows feature men's and women's nudity, appearing and disappearing in various semi-openings or through fine lace borders. Undergarments are taking over the city, in accordance with the presumptuous view that uncovering certain lower layers brings us closer to the fundamentals; closer to the reality of the self, into the simplicity of daily life, surrounded by intimacy. French has the expression *être dans son plus simple appareil* ('to be in your birthday suit'). The designer Lagerfeld believes there's a fashion trend inexorably on the way that will unveil what is most intimate. On the other hand, intimacy unveiled actually loses some of its value. In being made public, it undergoes a transformation. The process is complex: first, the uniqueness of the image or the new metaphor makes it deeply attractive; subsequently, use renders both image and word trite. Again, this is a process observable when private feelings are made public, and leads one to believe that life story takes a narrative turn from the moment the intent to expose governs the unveiling (and, likely, suggests necessary coverings).

In my own mind, the allusive examination of this transformation through a conversation with myself unfolds in a cultural patchwork of collective and individual memories. My life story gathers around the narrative of my thoughts. My willed resistance to the temptation of structure, structure that would misleadingly suggest a definitive truth has been unveiled, guides the controlled drift of conceptual connections, seeking legitimation, that I am consigning to the page. This is attributive, qualifying reflection, on the narrow frontier between the enstoried life and narrative.

Is it acceptable for a scholarly text to make use of breaks and flashbacks, metaphor and allusion, with all the authority of fiction? Here is the heart of the matter: how far will the qualitative approach dare to go in challenging the arrogation of legitimacy by the objective? If the reader can only make the text comprehensible at the cost of establishing connections with his or her own past, the reader-subject is transferred onto the object of the text. With the narrative form, greater comprehensibility could be hinted at, if need be, in the unveiling of the earliest seeds of the author's experience – even for the author of a qualitative research text. Are we prepared to accept the author-researcher's change in status from participatory researcher to a catalyst of discourse, one who deconstructs the interpretive connections that bring him or her to read his/her own work in the reader's stead? Are we prepared to accept the author-researcher's becoming a life-text researcher approximating his/ her own text, the text of a chapter being built up through embedding, like a life story constructed under the eye of the reader, without the creation of conceptualizing distance? Without predigesting a prerequisite organization of the discursive structures? But *can* the will to narrate be spontaneous?

Are we prepared to accept the researcher's becoming an author and thereby becoming committed to a reverse, 'other' organization of the text, to an organization that is underhand, elusive, that acts as an artist,

that convinces through the effects of art, but by depiction, not description? We should then be working at narrative transformation, which
imparts to the discourse produced a truth-to-life that is greater than that
of reality. This is the process whereby, a few decades ago, the fictional
studio reconstruction of episodes of war yielded a superior television
image of atrocities in Vietnam than films authentically made on the spot
could do. One television network was condemned for having manufactured reports that were more real than real life. Following a parallel line
of reasoning, certain critical historians refer to the novelist Honoré de
Balzac, who wrote *The Human Comedy,* as an ethnologist of the mores of
his era. He didn't require his subjects to sign research consent forms; he
simply hid their identities by conferring near-mythic stature upon them.

Winnipeg, 4 May 1993

I have been exiled to Quebec. Is Quebec in exile from Canada? Have I
become Canadian? Shall I become American? Does a label relating to
nationality represent a personality trait? A Swiss weekly accuses Alain
Tanner of being in thrall to another person. This would mean that he's
'under the influence' of a woman who has so thoroughly subjugated him
that she forced him to force the public to take part in a disturbing
voyeurism. The woman, then, violated the viewer, and the filmmaker
acted as pander. Yet the woman herself felt she had been violated. Who is
responsible here? This woman got drunk because of an anticipatory
violation by the gaze of a still-absent viewer.

The notions of narrative and life story make me think of a truly
constructed phenomenon, that of the stage-setting. Stage-settings recon-
struct the times and places of life in a series of differentiated representations. For instance, the ones I'm setting up right now with my intent to
'go public' with this journal. The times and places I'm reporting on are
different in their perspective from the times and places truly experienced. For example, right now I am conducting classroom observations
in Manitoba; at the same time, I live in Quebec, without quite being in
Canada.[2] Thus I manipulate several present tenses, several ecosystems
for my presence to the act of writing. These present-tense contexts
constitute my own present tense as a totality, but the moment I seek to
report on them by identifying their connections, I am faced with the
necessity of laying out, in linear fashion through a series of sentences, a
phenomenon that I experience as a simultaneity. While narrative represents an abstraction from lived experience, it does violence to reality in

order to better convey reality's characteristics. But if we confront the embeddedness of the points of view represented, we recognize the paradoxes inherent in writing, contradictions that reveal the flaw in narrative transformation. When I say 'flaw,' I mean in the sense of 'the flaw in the armour.' The obverse of narrative transformation is seen in the improbabilities and the inevitably biased perspectives imposed by linear transcription. I said, for instance, that I was conducting classroom observation. When I observe a class, I can't write. Since I must be writing (seeing that someone is reading me right now), I cannot be in class. Where am I?

Am I writing as an author or as a fictional narrator, stripped of all historical responsibility? Is my life story unfolding under my fingers, under your eyes, or am I merely lengthening lines, making lacework out of ink to cover the nakedness of the page? What power do my words have? Who is reading them, and do they resonate in his/her head? In his/her head-of-a-reader, in your head. Your head, watching you as you read my words. What impact do words have, can words have, on an individual, on the public? Will every reader hang on till the end of the chapter? How can I hit you qualitatively, reader, so that what I say will touch your life? Pierce your world – get you where you live?

But maybe in my life story it's more important, whoever the reader may be – and I'm not ignoring the fact that you're reading me – to add an item to my c.v. One more notch on the butt of the revolver. I'd simply be poised to shoot down one more chapter. If that were the case, this narrative would take on the appearance of a journal, in order to better disguise this particular aspect of my life story. I would be a qualitative researcher/quality-seeker – in large quantities. But you have just noticed the conditional mood: you suspect that in spite of everything I'm intent on not distancing this narrative too much from my own personal history, from a certain lived truth, at least the position I wish you to understand. With every line I myself surprise you in the act of assessing the text's authenticity. My authenticity as an author. Does that mean the life story touches you more than the narrative? But life story can be rather bland. Isn't what you really want to devour a narrative with all the appearance of a life story? Right there, behind your eyes, to devour happenings and thoughts that are after all terribly like your own? This man thinks the way I do (yet he is Swiss, and moreover he lives in Quebec). The story he's telling is your own story, which you haven't had the time to write. You were probably busy counting up frequencies.

You are playing the role of a peer in our joint reading of my text inside your head. We are engaged in recorded/deferred dialogue. Necessarily therefore, my life story becomes a small part of your own story. Even if you didn't really wish it (perhaps you're in the waiting room at the school board offices), I'm there, in the process of getting inside your head. For me in the act of writing, you too are a deferred and different being. I am speaking to you and imagining your reactions. Just as if we were in class, I'm watching your virtual reactions. I want you to know that at the first sign of boredom from you, I change, I adapt. I'm bent on keeping you there till the end of the chapter. You, there in my imagination, become a living part of my life story. My life story forms an integral part of what I am living and building inside my head, which I could never subject to the verdict of the public in a personal narrative. Which, more precisely, I could never have enough time or space to solidify under the eye of a reader.

My representation of you to a large extent entails your acceptance or rejection of the theses I am presenting and the form I present them in. And bear in mind that a part of my representation of you depends on the image I have of the university press that is publishing this text. I've already internalized standards of acceptance or rejection and I feel it distinctly when I reach the danger point. To an extent, I mould my narrative around these standards; clearly, my life story could never fit within these constraints. I am striving to stay within the limits of what is acceptable so that I can fit a maximum proportion of my life story into this narrative. My narrative, then, is coherent (oh yes, yes it is; read the chapter twice, you'll find it more coherent than you first thought; in fact, let's all stop a moment and see how you define coherence). N.B.: It's surprising how often you can stop in mid-reading; you weren't following any longer. Look at all the effort you're putting me to. Who was talking about coherence just now?

Now that 'narrative' has acquired a certain legitimacy, we can boast of it and send narratives to scholarly publications. In the social sciences we've recently witnessed a return to the human. But in spite of everything, in the course of this process of legitimation, the editorial committee responsible for assessing submissions remains more important than the targeted public. The editorial committee and its readers subscribe to a notion of the scientific that they legitimize with each new book. If the life story is already at a remove from the published text because a published text must be constructed so that it will reach its designated audience, who is to decide that one narrative is more truthful than another? What editor would dare to present, in the pages of a scholarly journal, the crisis of competence experienced by a researcher at the boundaries of qualitative research, if the editor suspected this personal story of being indeed just a story? The degree of conformity with reality remains the illusory criterion on which referees' judgments rest, value judgments, if it comes to that. Let's put the question another way: can a postmodern researcher allow herself or himself to reach a scholarly audience by constructing a narrative that represents empirical reality through metaphorical representativeness alone? Building representativeness would then become one of the necessary constructs of the social sciences. The social sciences would disappear in a patchwork of patterns of typicality.

The digression is closed. Supposing this research log is published, that is, supposing my representation of the legitimacy of this text fits within the limits of acceptability, or even desirability, as perceived by a sufficient number of the editors and readers to tip the balance in my favour; then by virtue of being published, the chapter would leave a conceptual legacy. It would constitute a precedent and other authors might believe, in their turn, that this type of unveiling/covering-over in the form of a hesitant waltz between life story and narrative is readable and judgeable. Now at this point in our discussion, you'll interrupt me and bring to my attention the fact that, seeing the text was accepted, I should have removed the conditional mood. Please note that I may have left it in to convey a sense of a tense in which the text existed 'before refereeing.' At this stage I could insert a few Proustian lines into this chapter, indicating the embedding of two temporal orders within my narrative of experience: the time of initial writing, the writing of my first journal; and the time of second writing, the writing/rereading of my own journal. But what if the lines you read are not positioned as epigraphs, like the little notations Proust added in rereading his work? What if these post-referee notes were really composed before the refereeing? Perhaps you will say I am subjecting the editorial committee to a very difficult trial. You could also say that in that case you would have before you irrefutable proof that I have constructed fiction that is suddenly distanced from my life story. Wouldn't my imagined anticipations then be a part of my life? The things you say make me think of William James's remark on the subject of batrachians. 'If I were a frog,' he maintained, 'I would exclaim, "No, I am myself, just myself."'

Writing about oneself, then, is scrutinized in light of standards of plural legitimacy that allow or prohibit publication. Paradoxically, it would be easier to publish a coherent narrative than the complexity of a life story, with all its jumble of temporal ruptures, intermingled spaces, flashbacks and flash-forwards, allusive constructions, and seemingly in-significant ideations. Thanks to your help, I shall just be able to manage to demonstrate that the absence of coherence in a narrative is a sign of truth telling. Narrative and life story are on a continuum: the frontier between them is diaphanous.

Are representativity and truth telling manufactured? Am I putting together a scenario? Have I fashioned a stage set? Am I in process of setting forth a fluid plot against a preconceived spatio-temporal back-ground, in which the clandestine relations and the advanced organizers would only emerge at the outcome of the debate, the debate with the you that is me?

Is good taste a factor in good narrative research? If it is possible for the life story to be in bad taste, won't the narrative approach tend towards smoothing the rough edges, sweetening reality for the sake of the image? When a stage set is put up, everything behind the scenes is hidden. Perhaps narrative, in contrast to the life story, has a merely illustrative value. After all, who would wish to describe reality as it truly is – who would benefit from it? Who can do it? The life story, then, may possibly also be manufactured: we make ourselves out to be heroes when in fact we felt we were cowardly, rattled, scared, and useless. The creature is manufactured; words constitute a show, a representation. Identity would seem to be constructed; Alain Tanner is under the influence.

Alain accepted that an actress should do everything inside his narra-tive, that her life story should become his narrative and that her narra-tive should become his life story. And the actress got drunk for the first time. But wasn't money a prime motive? The financial motive, then, partly differentiates life story from the public purpose of exhibitory narrative. In contrast to biography, qualitative research, while it may justify a salary, is scarcely profitable to the author. Unless it brings a measure of fame that would earn the academic author censure before long, the rewards of narrative authorship with scholarly pretensions are not financial.

Does this mean that objectivity is of interest to fewer people? To interest people, must we weave our cloth from myth and romance and pass from casual life story to the durability of fiction, exemplary fiction? Impressive words would carry all the more conviction for masking the ugliness of the intentions that shape their use: the appetite for power and money translated into exemplary tales, edifying instructions, pure words. Depending on the point of view, the removal of body hair trans-lates as empowerment or greed, aestheticism or crassness, love or debauchery, the victory of colour over line or the struggle between light and dark. True, in a post-structural analysis such dichotomies melt before this conversational argument: the narrative is the world, the world the narrative we construct from it. In Tanner's world, woman is identical with his fiction, with her fiction; Tanner is a social anthropologist. The exemplariness of the event transforms the life represented into a learning experience. Tanner is an educational researcher. It's a case of very special education.

I was contacted by the community of Swiss immigrants to Canada. They publish their newsletter in two languages: French and English. When a German-speaking Swiss researcher meets a French-speaking Swiss researcher, they communicate in English. I refused to join the Swiss-Canadian club because melted cheese gives me an upset stomach. But that was just a pretext. I don't really identify much with Switzerland any more; it's drifting farther away in my memories. I'm building myself an un-country, an everyplace where it feels good to live without belonging, where discrimination becomes difficult. At any rate, that's the narrative I recount to myself.

My life story is more painful. I left Switzerland so I could have the right to a voice within the world of academia. I wanted to sign my name to my ideas. I worked very hard for a long time to reach a stage where I can now allow others their own voices, and perhaps deceive myself that I'm one gatekeeper among others, or rather a guard over open doors. We guards who watch over open doors recognize each other instinctively as members of the same rainbow-coloured race. But hold it, I'm writing too well; my story is becoming a narrative and I'll be accused of embellishment. Does everyone understand that heaping up all sorts of colours makes white, was the message suitably slanted? As I was saying, the risk involved in mutual recognition is that unavowed networking within an interest group may become invisible lobbying. Tomorrow, Tanner's friends may all be sharing their most intimate experiences and they'll have forgotten the liberatory effect that first gesture may have had. Interest groups seem to destroy meaning by widening its currency.

Re-cognitional Post-structures

A narrative needs no comment, for it is itself a comment on life.
Seeking for hidden structural information helps preserve the mind from laziness.

CHAPTER FOUR

Exploring Educational Spaces: Mythic Territories of Experience-Sharing

My deconstruction of some trends specific to teacher education in chapters 1 and 2 enlightened some paradoxes, and demonstrated the primacy of experience. Deconstruction should be followed by a reconstruction process. This is the goal of chapters 3, 4, and 5. What positive definition could we give to *teacherhood*? Rather than formulating a standardized definition based on teacher proficiency, I will consider this issue in a more philosophical light. For that purpose I will come back to the mythic, Indo-European roots of teaching discussed in the first chapter of the book, then I will develop a neo-Aristotelian definition of the essence of teacherhood. In an Aristotelian tradition, meaning is defined as a potential or actualized space of action and intelligence. The actualization of teacherhood in the dimension of time is but a manifestation of this potential mental space: it is a shared meaning-making process.

In this chapter[1] I offer a demonstration based on two premises. The first premise is that meaning is stratified into diverse epistemologies, or ways of knowing. There exist strata, levels, or – to use another metaphor – 'beams' of meaning analogous to a beam of white light comprising the spectrum of colours. In fact, I would go further and suggest that epistemic beams of meaning determine cultural and social currents. The second premise, which is neo-Aristotelian, defines meaning as the space of action and intelligence, whether potential or actualized. The demonstration: time is a manifestation of this mental space. This agrees with the theory of relativity, according to which time and space are reciprocal functions. Thus meaning is produced by the collision of intelligence with space and the reconstituted temporal sequentiality that results from this collision. Teacherhood works at this intersection.

In this perspective, spaces of meaning are stratified so that they establish congruence among participants of the same epistemic beam. Epistemic beams are distinguished by signs and people linked by a shared interactional system. The creation of this interactional, symbolic system, or of a linking metaphor, facilitates consensus and characterizes the acting mind. The acting mind is the active meaning that illuminates the passage to action from a state of potentiality, or, to use the term from scholastic philosophy, from a state *in posse*. Following a brief overview of the relation between territoriality and meaning in Indo-European and medieval cosmology and then in Edward Soja's postmodern geography, I examine teacherhood, the meaning relation that is established between teachers and students. I show how meaning beams are organized and how they determine both action and meaning. The acting mind is a theory that allows us to take account of the cultural terrains and symbolic substrata that differentiate human groups and regulate teaching, seen as a cultural transfer. Also it accounts for the living meaning-making processes that characterize teacherhood.

Virtual Space

Virtual spaces are meaning spaces: space produces meaning and, reciprocally, meaning constructs space. The virtuality of space is a current concept that has become familiar in the form of cyberspace. In fact, the concept of space as meaning corresponds to a very old tradition, passed from the Persians to the Greeks and then spread to the Arabs, before being reappropriated by medieval European theologians and then by the humanists, who ascribed a completely different significance to it – one that is not so distant from Edward Soja's reflections, which we will examine hereafter.

Going back to the Indo-European origins of this concept, we find that certain Vedic texts describe lived space poetically as the product of the channels of the senses. Since they underpin the universe, the senses have a constitutive power in creation. They are *devas*, intelligent beings that proceed from the first light and bring various functions together in the process of intelligence's self-manifestation. Georges Dumézil (1941), working in comparative grammar, has observed that the word *deva* contains the root *Iau*, which means 'light'; the same root is later found in the Greek word *Zeus* and the Latin *Jupiter* (in ancient Vedic, *Io Pita*, 'Father Light'). Vedic poetry is coded, each space term bearing a function as the representation of an aspect of the intelligence that underlies manifestation. For example, a cow is a symbol of fertility, energy, and abundance, easily understood in primitive societies, a symbol whose survival we see in the human geography of contemporary India. The proliferation of the cow is in fact proof, if proof were needed, of the impact of symbol systems on the spaces in which human life unfolds. Under the Vedic approach, creation and intelligence are inseparable, with the contact between the creature and the source of its manifestation requiring channels of communication, messages, and messengers; and the nature of this contact being a determining force in the human being's status. This developing status corresponds to phases of intelligence, translated into geographic space as eras of peace and fertility or periods of war and social antagonism. We will come back to this when we look at Soja's definition of war.

I said that traces of this Indo-European concept are to be found in the Middle Ages. In *L'intelligence collective: Pour une anthropologie du cyberspace*, Pierre Lévy (1997) traces the history of the concept. A certain Persian and Jewish theosophical tradition proposed a neo-Platonic reading of Aristotle.[2] This approach led to the spread, in the tenth-century Muslim world, of the concept of the acting mind. The acting mind was believed to link, through thought, human beings to each other and to God in a consciousness emerging from their collective exchanges. For Aristotle, God is pure action; the active intellect holds a central place in his philosophy. The cosmology of al-Farabi (872–950) and Avicenna (the Latin name for Ibn Sina, 980–1037) is closely linked to this concept. The process of knowing creates cosmological space: the world proceeds from experience, and levels of abstraction are imbricated in any perceptual space. In fact, they constitute knowledge. Beams of meaning are perceptual qualities constituted from experiential space. Human beings who achieve a vision of space enter into meaning, independently of time. These teachers, capable of perceiving time in space, come into contact with the moving principles of the world. They are then one with the acting mind, even while maintaining an intelligence distinct from the principle that that intelligence expresses. Thus, level by level, strata of consciousness are embodied in space, bestowing meaning on the dynamics of life. Consciousness has been interpreted in most related philosophical works as pertaining to the 'I' Enlightenment tradition, but it might be analysed as an integrated feature of life within a semiotic dimension (Tochon, 2002b).

In Avicennian tradition, the acting mind is a state of the mind, an 'angel.' In the light of these cultural sources, angels should be reinterpreted as constituents of lived meaning. As shocking as it may appear, interpreting meaning-making processes as the spirited enterprise and *ingenium* (engineering) that underlies and follows the deconstruction process is not a mixing of genres; it can enter a dialogical demonstration of the intertwined space and time of life narratives. In the demystification process, an increased awareness of hidden meanings is produced, which does not imply that meaning would be outside of the situations lived. I will pursue this analysis further. An angel is a very abstract, interactional – and possibly shared – meaning. For Avicenna, an angel is the coming together of souls in a collective meaning and direction, the tracing of the boundary of a moving intelligence. Angels are expressions of the acting mind, integrated beams of meaning. They give meaning to action, because they are the meaning of spaces and their movement. The passage to action, in the Aristotelian sense of being born into intelligence, is the issuance of meaning and a merging with the epistemic beam that, manifesting the acting mind, gives meaning. Space constitutes virtual action, which is actualized only when the acting mind becomes aware of its own movement. Space in potentiality (possible space) becomes space in action (real space) when it is inhabited by shared consciousness. Thus space acquires a new dimension when the acting mind is actualized within it. This leads me to refer metaphorically to teaching as a manifestation of the acting mind, because teacherhood plays an essential role in remembering the nature of action. Teaching is a transfer of the acting mind; in a sense, it *is* the acting mind. It realizes its meaning. Consciousness of the act as an expression of the mind transforms space into a meaningful situation. That space, linked by the mind to collective thought, resonates with spaces being moved in other places and by similar dynamics. This epistemic synergy adds meaning to space, a phenomenon that can be termed an irradiation by the meaning for which the acting mind is both receiver and sender. A merging with the meaning of the space confers the power of understanding and meaningful action. From this epistemic contemplation are born all forms of knowledge. Contact with space can only become real by reason of contact with the mind. This sums up the philosophy of the Aristotelian Avicenna.

A century after the death of Avicenna, this perspective was extended to include multiple relations between meaning spaces. In the twelfth century, Abu'l-Barakat al-Baghdadi described multiple epistemic personalities, something Avicenna had not done. According to this later concept, space in potentiality is actualized by groupings of souls whose acting mind moulds human orientations, trajectories, and geography.

This concept postulates the existence of plural individual geographies linked by networks of shared meaning. Families of the mind share a certain meaning of the real and radiate the meaning of one particular acting mind through the space that has become action.

Humanism transformed these mind spaces into cultural spaces. The humanist project has meaning emerge from the foundation. Light is born of a community of standardized meaning. In this view, space is centripetal and ascending, whereas before it was conceived as centrifugal and descending. The sources of meaning are perceived as immanent, springing forth from the human when the human approaches the human, and recognizes in it its own human identity. Evil, then, is the absence of communication, the turning in on oneself, a reason for excommunication from the group. In this one can discern certain premises of the Frankfurt school, Habermas's communicative action being perhaps no more than a neo-Aristotelian recursion. Knowledge from above is replaced by a horizontal, shared knowledge; intelligence is the act of communication and emerges from reciprocity and not from an external intelligence. Beams of interest distinguish human groups. Is this a matter of intellectual tribalism? Human beings take sustenance from cultural beams that assign them to a social space (Lather & Smithies, 1997). In the Renaissance, medieval clannishness was transformed into cultural schools, schools of thought, and schools of the arts; plurality came to be seen as an enrichment of the human heritage. Thus humanism offered a transfigured version of clannishness, according to which membership was dictated by noble inclinations whose manifestations allow for the actualization of the most refined aspects of intelligence and taste. The humanists appropriated space and transfigured it, for example in the sphere of architecture. Teacherhood is the understanding of the meaning given to space in time. Through teaching, contact with the origins becomes a life narrative.

The Influence of the Acting Mind on Manifestation

In this attempt at defining the nature of teaching, how does the contact that characterizes teacherhood become operational? What is the link between virtual meaning spaces and humans in search of mutual contact? How does the acting mind manifest itself? One medium is orality, the oral language. Here *language* must be understood in a philosophical, as well as semiotic sense: the word or speech, and its symbolic transfer. Working within this long tradition in the philosophy of language, Wilhelm von Humboldt (1936/1974) proposed the principle of the correlation of forms within the functional unity of human life. For him, the interior form of language constitutes the dynamic giving of form to the mind. The internal meaning of language is immanent; it gathers together the silent impulses of a language category belonging to a founding group. The individual being, whether a person or a nation-state, is actualized as an expression and coming into effect of the energy that has engendered it. The mind is thus bound in loyalty to perceptible space and to those intellectual energies that ally themselves with the vitality of the imagination of the senses. The actualization of meaning through the power of language, according to this view, causes the sphere of the universe's virtual contents *(Vorstellung)* to pass into the perceptible space of its representation and dynamic implementation *(Darstellung)*. This process situates teaching. Since representation is a passage to action and learning *(Bildung)*, it also leads from education to the moulding of character *(Formung,* or *form-*action). In this perspective, a symbol is the threshold manifestation of a linguistic fact. 'Language is an action, it manifests the truly creative initiative of the mind; and in each language this action designates the heart of its individuation, the hearth of its manifestations' (p. 364). For example, there exists a 'correlation between the interior form of thought and the phonetic component ... [This synthesis] presupposes a truly creative action of the mind' (p. 365). Thus the instrument of teaching is language: language expressions stimulate the contact with the mind underlying symbols through form-actions. Teacherhood is empowered by the consciousness of the correlation between action and the mind, the consciousness that stimulates the contact. And the contact that characterizes teacherhood becomes operational through oral interactions supported with the awareness of the meaning of action. The oral touch conveys the acting mind and defines teaching.

The principle of correlation was well known in medieval scholarship; Eco (1992) refers to it when examining cosmological signatures. The mind is conveyed through language, which mediates the relationship with nature. Variations of language indicate variations of mind corresponding to geographic specifics. In von Humboldt's time, German linguists were sure they had identified the *Ursprache* – the mother of all languages – in Sanskrit. A little later, the existence of ancient Vedic was discovered. In Vedic and Sanskrit texts, as well as the various denatured traditions analysed by Eco (1992), one sees traces of the notion *that linguistic facts are determined by geography and model inhabitants' minds.* Like the links to be observed, according to the notion of microcosmic/macrocosmic correspondence, between what is above and what is below, the spirit of a place dictates the lifestyles, language, and customs of those living in a given region. That this notion had been bequeathed to the German philosophers and linguists of von Humboldt's day is to be explained by the rediscovery of Sanskrit, whose near-perfect grammatical description by Panini suggested an artificial language or one divinely generated. Sanskrit is not the only language to have given rise to such speculation: according to Kabbalistic thought, Hebrew harbours a secret numerology that makes it possible to understand the universe. Traditional Chinese writing also corresponds to cosmological principles. Von Humboldt found traces of this principle of correspondence (or correlation) in some twenty cultures and languages, from Javanese Kavi to Angolan Bundu, from Persian Zend to Inca Quechua, from the Mayan languages of the Yucatan to the Cherokee of the Carolinas. Edward Sapir made cautious use of some of von Humboldt's postulates in his observations on the influence of the environment on language. In his opinion, the physical environment is only reflected in language to the extent that it has been influenced by social factors (Sapir, 1989, p. 74). Thus, a reference to something from the physical sphere implies that the linguistic group has reached an agreement on its existence and on the interest that it represents. In this situation the influence is to be found in the content, the vocabulary, the phonetics, or the morphology. Social institutions are themselves constantly creatively influenced, revived, or reaffirmed by individual communicative acts exchanged by the group's members (p. 91). The mind of these individual actions attests to their potential for social change, through language and teacherhood.

The relationship between environment, mental models, and language is in fact the subject of one chapter of Thomas Sebeok's 1991 book, *A Sign Is Just a Sign*, the chapter called 'In What Sense Is Language a Primary Modeling System?' Here, Sebeok takes up anew the propositions he had put forward in 1970 at the Moscow-Tartu School with Ivanov: 'The notion of a secondary modeling system in the broad sense refers to an ideological model of the world where the environment stands in reciprocal relationship with some other system, such as an individual organism, a collectivity, a computer, or the like, and where its reflection functions as control of this system's total mode of communication. A model of the world thus constitutes a program for the behavior of the individual, the collectivity, the machine, etc., since it defines its choice of operations, as well as the rules and motivations underlying them' (p. 49). Sebeok then writes that human productions, institutions, and the movements of civilizations are moulded by such models, or *Umwelten.* As the chapter unfolds, he addresses the relationship between this *Umwelt* and perceptual activity: the model has an impact on the perceptible world and on nature. True, language evolved as a primary form of adaptation to the environment, but today, as Sebeok would have us understand, language must be understood to be a secondary modelling system, as opposed, for example, to endosemiotic models such as the genetic, immune, and neural codes.

Considering mental models as signs in the Peircian sense nevertheless implies neo-Platonic top-down modelling (Sebeok, 1991, p. 57), which is very different from the perspective of Edward Soja, who describes the relational, creative role of material proximity in the modelling of social equilibrium, for example. As for von Humboldt, for Soja geography has an impact on form, expressive potential, and the psyche. In von Humboldt, however, this impact is born of a functional unity within which entities and meanings pass from virtuality to representational actualization.

The Acting Mind of Teaching, or the Spatialization of History

Let us situate teacherhood in a postmodern space. If, for humanism, evil consists in the absence of communication, how has modernity found the means to place people in communication with each other and what are the inevitable paradoxes in the geography of communication? Edward Soja has analysed these and proposes their postmodern transcendence. What follows is a brief history of postmodern geographies in Soja's oeuvre.

It is hard to trace Soja in databases, because he is swamped by a profusion of articles in the agrifood disciplines. His name covers enormous economic space. Nevertheless, following a few clues it is possible to recover two periods of time: one outstanding set of works is clustered in the 1970s, following his PhD from Syracuse, when he was assistant professor at Northwestern University; a second group occurs in the years 1989–96 and constitutes the main focus of attention here. Soja thought in interdisciplinary terms very early on, examining geographical problems within the context of the interrelation of the social, the economic, and the political, moved by the will to transcend the existing dichotomy between the reign of quantity and the reign of quality (or of description, to use his term). This integrative change arose within a quest for values, values whose origins, Soja concedes, are difficult to trace.

In 1968, Soja broached the geography of modernization in examining the origins of a nation in Kenya. The territory in question was defined before colonization, which Soja describes as a penetration of the fertile fabric of traditional African society. The intrusion of colonization created a European island in an African sea and initiated a transition manifested in considerable changes in the society's modes of communication. Transport and communications took on modern structures, giving modernity a spatial dimension and giving primacy to the Kikuyu people largely by reason of their geographic proximity to the major European centres, including Nairobi. Thus history and geography mingled, with the highlands' sphere of influence corresponding to urbanization and underpinning the subsystems of modernization. 'The imprint of colonial penetration and the establishment of effective administrative control temporarily froze the pre-European cultural geography, and Kenya was compartmentalized into a series of European and African reserves' (Soja, 1968, p. 101). Together, economics and education drew the African out of traditional spaces into a broad and powerful network of communications. However, 'Geographic proximity and accessibility to the major modes and flow lines within the new circulatory system affected the degree to which various people were transformed by the processes of change' (ibid.). Considering the factors that contributed to modernity in spatial terms, Soja analysed this flow of new meaning by means of principal component analyses.

The next book of Edward Soja's that I was able to find is called *The African Experience: Vol. 2, Syllabus*, written with John Paden (Paden & Soja, 1970). The book reviews the essential aspects of ethnic culture, from family and kinship to the arts and music. It presents racial resistance as articulated against a background of slavery and examines the impact of colonialism under the aspect of changes in the African character. African nationalisms and pan-African supranationalism form the context of both religious and political issues. African creativity is exported abroad; links to French culture and African American ethnicity allow for a return to both temporal and spatial origins and the identificational reconquest of the substratum shared with these. Here the aim is to have African identity recognized outside the continent, not in the superficial way represented by the 'proliferation of poor imitation art, often crudely executed and highly commercialized (such as the airport curios which have been imported in increasing numbers to

Europe and America)' (p. 360), but in a deep way, the way of the awakening of Black consciousness. Self-imposed personal exiles such as James Baldwin's in Paris are analysed.

In 1970, Edward Soja received a grant from the National Science Foundation that led to the 1971 publication by the Association of American Geographers of a small work, *The Political Organization of Space*. Soja's original conceptualization of human territoriality begins in earnest with this work. He traces its foundations in Aristotelian logic and Greek geometry: the nation-state founded on the Euclidean properties of space imposes the concept of territorial belonging on the world. Unlike previous societies, the Greeks subjected space to the concept of territorial identity. War resulted from this expansionist concept, since the Western world was not yet aware of methods of imposing cultural influence without invading the physical space of the other. War is defined through the application of the principles that the identity of nations rests on. Soja's analysis shows the extent to which influence is conveyed through communication. Consequently, he considers it possible to find substitutes for war, 'whatever functions war may serve' (1971, p. 32).

Thus Soja proposes a framework for geographical analysis, resituating the concept of boundaries: 'Each human being creates his own "activity space" which becomes the context for his most detailed knowledge of his environment and within which most of his daily activities are regularly carried out. At the most micro-scale, each individual surrounds himself with a portable series of spaces, or personal distance zones, "bubbles" which guide and shape his interaction with other individuals. Thus without formal boundaries, space becomes organized and structured into focal points, core areas, networks of interaction, domains, spheres of influence, hinterlands, buffer zones, no-man's-lands, cultural homelands, regions, neighborhoods, gang "turfs", and ghettos' (1971, p. 1).

Soja refuses to replace the old orthodoxy with a new one. He seeks to explore the political organization of space: the ways that interaction structures space for the fulfilment of political functions. To this end he studies methods of urban categorization in Kenya, Sunderland, and Los Angeles. Because his perspective becomes anthropological, he examines the importance of territoriality in the animal kingdom. Its purposes include safety, protection, and the regulation of the density of occupation of space. Animal territorial concerns also aim towards the structuring and cohesion of the group, thus balancing the social forces of cooperation, conflict, and competition. Animal territoriality emerges from dominance behaviours, which translate social position into space.

Movements and the field of action indicate the power for influence of an animal organism. This is equally true for human microterritorial bubbles, as suggested in Edward Hall's studies in proxemics in *The Silent Language* (1959). It can be argued that the notion of private property flows from territoriality in this sense. Nevertheless, in the case of human macroterritoriality, it may be conceived that social territoriality is cultural above all.

In his 1989 book, *Postmodern Geographies: The Reassertion of Space in Critical Social Theory*, Edward Soja reduces time to space and denounces the historical perspective and 'the despatializing distortions of historicism' (p. 7). His preface, while located at the start of the book, is a postscript that ironically demonstrates how the segmentation of space can come up against the axis of time. Soja revisits a series of postmodern authors and cuts himself off definitively from 'Cartesian cartography' (ibid.) He proposes 'a social ontology in which space matters from the very beginning' (ibid.), which rises up against the silences of history. According to Soja, this spatialization constitutes a transcendence of the temporal concepts that influenced both Heideggerian and Sartrian ontology and Anthony Giddens's (1981) processing of space and time.

Although Soja argues, in the spirit of Foucault (1986), that time is not dead, he emphasizes space over time. The hegemonic obsession with history has tended to occlude and foreclose the role of space in social life. Even Marxism required a metacritique in order to advance from its orthodox historicism and spatial fixity – which is a kind of absolutism and overgeneralization – and reassert spatial praxis and human geographies. Despite his insistence on space, Soja's position is not one of spatial fetishism or hyperterritorialism. Rather, it aims to increase the consciousness of space and synchrony at the intersection of enactments of the acting mind. There is a political dimension to space: space is where actions and substance acquire meaning. The deconstruction of historicism leads to a strategic reconstruction of space and a passage from resistance to flexible specialization and differentiation (Soja, 1989, p. 74).

Soja proposes a sociospatial dialectic that becomes trialectic in his 1996 book on Thirdspace. There is a 'distinction between space *per se,* space as a contextual given, and socially-based spatiality, the created space of social organization and production' (1989, p. 79). Whereas time and space were linked by light in the Indo-European and Avicennian cosmology, the human geography of Soja links time, space, and matter. Ironically, though he would take a postmodern stance, Soja's physical vision of space and matter corresponds to modernist canons, or rather to prequantum physics. A quantum physics of space designates the energetic and light sources of matter in terms of wave functions and photonic light (Jahn & Dunne, 1987). Soja's conception, in contrast, is neo-Avicennian: he shows how nature, understood as the context of life, models enminded nature-in-action and predetermines human relationships. Organized space gives rise to intelligent strata. It is interesting to see that in the revisionist view of Castells (1977, p. 115, cited by Soja, 1989, p. 83), 'space is a material product,' as it was in the Indo-European tradition of the *varnas*, where space or ether was the fifth element that made possible the sense of hearing. Both rely on the assumption of a pre-existing law governing a thing's existence as object and the transformation of such existence. In the present text space is defined as a relational substance.

The 'historical geography' of social systems provides strong evidence that the 'transformations of the spatio-temporal matrices ... are the real substratum of mythical, religious, philosophical or "experiential" representations of space-time' (Poulantzas, 1978, p. 26, cited by Soja, 1989, p. 118). This view matches Wilhelm von Humboldt's perspective (1936/ 1974): for him, geography was a determining constituent of the mind and explained language, culture, and society.

Culturally speaking, the territories of towns and nations are divided. These geographical divisions have a social meaning: each division represents a stratum of society. But the space that determines identity has changed its meaning in postmodern civilization: telecommunications have conferred spatial ubiquity on it. It is therefore now based on a politicization of interterritorial communication. This logic achieves a fascinating extension in cyberspace, and I am tempted to go one step further and argue that cyberspace is the point of passage to semiotic territoriality. We are in the process of passing from a static definition of territoriality to a dynamics of culture in which conceptual boundaries acquire political meaning. Thematic angels are blanketing the planet and bringing together cultural groups.

As Soja shows, spatial identity is affirmed through methods of communication and in the zones where we communicate. But currently, geographic regionalisms are being replaced by conceptual regionalisms. The sense of exclusivity that characterizes social territoriality is taking on a thematic allure. In one sense it could be said that clannishness is being reborn to the detriment of the nation-state, and the semiotics of worldwide human relations are taking on a tribal appearance. In the postmodern world, there are no more castes. Instead, we have honey-combs in virtual beehives, humming with conceptual nutriment (such as Web pages crammed with information and the offer of services). These location-less hives belong to no national territory and their shared spaces are henceforward immaterial. Within these cultural enclaves, these communications ghettos, belonging is displayed by means of clusters of tastes, colours, vocabularies, lures, and molar behaviours that allow for a mutual recognition lying beyond and below the official structures of public meaning. They are one with the beams of Avicenna's acting mind. Public meaning has now become the property of lobbies seeking to win back powers of intercommunication while distancing their thematic networks from the systematic co-opting of their key concepts for economic purposes.

Semiotic Territoriality in the World of the School

In his latest work, Soja (1996) develops the trialectical ontology of Henri Lefebvre (1991) (historical, spatial, social) into a trialectics of space: lived, perceived, conceived. Thirdspace is a space of representation made of images, signs, and symbols. It inherits the Kantian space of abstraction and the phenomenological space of perception (Merleau-Ponty, 1962; Primozic, 2001). The spatial ontology, or spatiology, of Lefebvre constitutes an effort to escape Cartesian dualism, whose 'stubborn bi-polarity' (Soja, 1996, p. 36) prohibits the conciliation of materialism with idealism. Otherness is the focus in Thirdspace, and the analytical space is the social space of the everyday. '*Everything* comes together in Thirdspace: subjectivity and objectivity, the abstract and the concrete, the real and the imagined, the knowable and the unimaginable, the repetitive and the differential, structure and agency, mind and body, consciousness and the unconscious, the disciplined and the transdisciplinary, everyday life and unending story' (Soja, 1996, pp. 56–7).

In the remainder of this text, using the reflective journal that I wrote up in 1993 during classroom observations (see chapter 3), I would like to examine how the concepts of semiotic territoriality and meaning beams can be actualized. How does space divide functional units with their differences, both political and epistemic? How do networks of communication and noncommunication within a classroom explain cultural strata, those cultural strata that prevent some human beings from encountering each other conceptually despite their geographic proximity? Here are some mental spaces that enlightened me when I was conducting classroom research in Manitoba. I will not discuss them analytically: as I explained in the previous chapter, a narrative needs no comment, for it is in itself a comment on life. I hope seeking for hidden structural information will help preserve the necessary mindset for reader-researchers in action poetry, as will be seen in chapter 5.

Case 1

The first case illustrates perception of a connection between interior reflection, or the 'acting mind' of a situation, and the events that unfolded within it.

Research Journal – 5 May 1993

This morning, while observing the class, I noticed a girl student wearing a long, pretty, flowered dress beneath which protruded jeans and hiking boots. At first, I thought some genius of the fashion world had had the notion of freeing the human form from the shackles created by our daily choice of our clothed appearance. With the balance between animus and anima restored, soon men and women would free themselves by submitting to the newly imposed fashion order, and all wear heavy jeans and light dresses. But while we were eating, a friend of mine opposed this view. For her, the dress worn over jeans represented the first stage in a return to femininity. This friend explained that in her experience, when you're used to wearing jeans you feel terribly naked under a dress. Dress-over-jeans, then, would be Phase 1 in preparation for Phase 2, and Phase 2 implies you take off the jeans. As it was most unusual at that time, the jeans-dress gave me a salty-sweet sensation.

The research I'm doing is not related to students' dress habits, but this does represent one of the many components of the complex classroom environment. When I come into the classroom, some teachers introduce me to their pupils and some don't. Before long, I become part of the furniture. Then our experiences blend in a dialogue between present and past, among the evocative aspects of classroom events that reverberate through my storehouse of theories, anecdotes, lived experience, and memories. Phenomenologically, two stories are entangled in each other: the story of the classroom events, and my life story. This entanglement, which Clandinin and Connelly (1989a) described using the sound-based metaphor of narrative rhythm, takes the form in my own life of basting, of the somewhat slack stitching between the weft of my life and the embroidery of events. Using a metaphor from Mallarmé, I distinguish between the broad, flaxen thread of life and the lacework of the narrative I make of life when I write. Mallarmé the poet embroidered words, the lace of memory, onto the white paper. Mallarmé the translator reconstructed the universe of Edgar Allan Poe in French. An author transfers universes onto pages.

This afternoon (I transfer the universe of the present tense onto these pages) the students, fourteen-year-olds, are rehearsing sketches. I've got a little time to write, because the different groups are getting ready. The teacher's strategy is to allow the students maximum liberty but yank them regularly back into line every ten minutes with two strident yells and a warning that she's writing on the blackboard. The students, well aware that this pattern is as reliable as a chronometer, suddenly (at the ninth minute) suggest to the teacher that she go out: this way, they'll be spared the impending yells. Supposedly, the principal has called her over the intercom and she didn't hear him. The strident shouts postponed, the first group starts performing its sketch. Since the teacher has gone out, the student teacher takes over. I am an absent spectator; I seem not to be a part of the network of meaning deployed by the class.

The sketch being staged by the group takes place in a clothing store. As far as I can tell, the teacher's aim in having the students do these sketches was to get them to use the imperative. The salesman orders the client to try on a suit. Taking advantage of the teacher's absence, the student playing the part of the client makes a big deal of getting undressed to try on the new garment. The students' eyes are all glued to the student teacher. How will she react? The student teacher seems to find the situation perfectly natural. The students seem disappointed; just then, the teacher comes back inside and utters three strident yells. A girl student raises her hand and waves three fingers. Two students break out laughing. The teacher puts three names on the blackboard. A student makes a show of adjusting her watch: she's getting ready for the countdown to the next two shouts.

This journal entry indicates the presence of physical elements in the classroom that are anticipated by my reflections: the noting of the dress-over-jeans is followed by an event related to this attainment of awareness (the de-jeansing as a social transformation). Similarly, my perception of the alternation, like an audible rhythm, between internal attention and external attention is followed by a rhythmic series of guttural spasms (the strident yells) on the part of the teacher, which suddenly form the object of a plot and become central to the students' strategy for nonlearning (or for extracurricular learning). As both Edward Hall (1983) and Henri Lefebvre (1991) have noted, some rhythms are worth analysing. Jung (1964) writes of synchronicity: we note a coincidence of a coming to awareness and events as though the human geography embraced the situation's acting mind, as if the meaning that a person emits in relation to a situation were shared semiotically by participants in the situation.

The idea here is not to suggest a mystical link between thought and situations, but to examine the congruence between the act of conceptualization and the quasi-physical sharing of events by a group of human beings, in the sense that the conceptual projection is capable of modelling collective action in line with a specific human geography. What is of interest is the examination of a case of correspondence in a semiotic light.

Let's look at the correspondence between coming to awareness and its effect on a given environment. To what extent does an internal conceptualization have a 'congruence effect' in that it elicits the emergence of corresponding situational occurrences? Could it be, for instance, that, somewhat the way André Breton's poem 'Nadja' foreshadowed a meeting years before it took place, thought organizes the semiotics of space and certain kinds of events follow? This is suggested by the correspondence between certain events recorded in this research journal, which yet demonstrate its atemporal nature:

1 My reflections on dresses/jeans are followed by a near-striptease in the classroom ('de-jeansing').
2 Recent reading of Edward Hall's work on certain rhythms leads me to note the rhythm of the teacher's yells; these yells lead the students to create a plot and then start to count the yells.
3 In case 3 below, the video about Amsterdam ties in with my upcoming trip to Amsterdam. Moreover, this journal entry was incorporated into the present chapter just before I opened Soja's book to the page that features photos and analyses of Amsterdam.

I am not supplying these illustrations with the aim of inducing magical thinking; the framework of this reflection is scientific. I wish to analyse correspondence phenomena under the aspect of the congruence of signs in the atemporal space of meaning, and contemplate scientifically the possible synchronicity (to resume a Jungian hypothesis) of events that imbue space with meaning.

Case 2

All human beings carry their geography with them, in von Humboldt's sense, in the form of an accent. The accent of a European francophone leads to immediate categorization by French-Canadian conversational partners; this accent is associated with cultural stereotypes (and in all likelihood the process of stereotyping is reciprocal and to some extent justified). Geographic labelling is also the product of visibility. In one sense, racial distinctions are partly linked to primary methods of perceptual categorization, with which certain kinds of affect and secondary elements are sometimes subsequently associated. In the journal entry that follows, both these phenomena are present, suggesting both the link between identity and geography and the primacy of enminded geography over physical geographies.

Research Journal – 6 May 1993

I am examining the narratives of adjustments made to language lesson plans, in cases where the adjustments relate to life stories. This morning I've been phoning school principals to arrange for data collection. The school boards have already given me the green light. Immersion schools are mostly anglophone, and welcome me. On the other hand, it's a privilege to get access to Manitoba's French schools: they are few and heavily solicited. From the moment I open my mouth, my European accent is remarked upon. Sensitivity to this seems to be less marked at the elementary and junior high levels than in high schools. The elite sectors of minority francophone communities aren't keen on a European showing up to give them language lessons, which is a perfectly natural feeling. One principal has been kind enough to invite me over, providing the explanation that his school community, being bilingual, is very tolerant. Later, to show me how tolerant he is respecting people from other parts of the francophone world, he calls over a student in the hallway and inquires after her Haitian family. This student, amazed, answers that her mother, a Canadian, separated from her Haitian husband when the girl was born. The girl was born in Canada.

Will I be accepted as a Canadian one day? When my presence is endowed with a normative impact in a francophone environment, I'm no longer the innocent observer, a furnishing among furnishings. My presence has political effect without my noticing it. Certain fears are allayed if I speak of my Swiss origins. Switzerland's francophones constitute 28 per cent of the population; they voted *for* Europe. Minority groups should support each other. In contrast, my position as an ex-European in a no-man's-land makes my relations with anglophone Canadians easier: if a European francophone is sometimes seen as potentially aggressive by North American francophones, she or he is, conversely, perceived as politically neutral by most of Canada's anglophones. His or her life story is not a story of language struggles.

Case 3

This case is an extension of the preceding one. Some aspects of this story are anchored in geographical location. Just as linguistic geography allows for the retracing of ancient strata, with innovations spreading outwards through space and time from creative centres, so certain diachronic aspects of culture seem to be fixed in space and perpetuate themselves locally, as though attached to a single semiotic beam.

Research Journal – 6 May 1993

This teacher introduced me to his colleagues with a slightly bitter joke: in a French school, I had spoken to him in English to ask him where visitor parking was. 'Now,' he says, 'people in Montreal are speaking English.' He offered me a coffee. For a long time before returning to teaching, he led a parents' association. He was a member of a pressure group. Now he is once more under pressure in his own classroom. He likes children in this age group (eleven to twelve years), because they enjoy learning and working. This morning, like every morning, the teacher starts his day with a dictation exercise, immediately after the national anthem and the Lord's Prayer. The dictation text is about the good old days in the Western plains. The children will ask questions about vocabulary and spelling, and then do peer correction of each other's work. Each pupil has a set place; they raise their hands for permission to speak. The power of digression belongs to the teacher; he assesses the pupils' tiredness and goes from spelling exercises to conjugation and grammar exercises according to their ability to take it in. When I have to leave the classroom to visit the next class, he breaks off and, taking his cue from the dictation text, he asks the pupils if they ever encountered a bear. Two boys, their interest suddenly aroused, raise their hands and want absolutely to recount their experiences.

In the class next door, a very different epistemology prevails. I leave behind homonym lists, past participle agreement, dictation, the forest and the bear in it, and enter a universe of movement and energy. The teacher is conducting a debate on human rights. Her course is solidly rooted in the resolution of day-to-day ethical problems in modern life. The children have recently read *Vincent and Me*, a biography of Van Gogh worked into a little girl's autobiography by means of the plot. In class, the debate revolves around the distinction between honesty and dishonesty. Now, the children are watching a video of the story they've just analysed. While the movie is running, for every character, they fill in a chart, specifying the character's honest and dishonest actions as events unfold. Most notably, the heroine paints so skilfully that a forger buys her charcoal sketches and sells them as real Van Goghs. The teacher points out how this shows that you can steal ideas or a name. It's a shame that only the formal aspect of ideas enjoys legal protection. The heroine rebels when her painting teacher reproaches her with not being herself, with just being a copyist. The fact is, the heroine shows such ingenuity in recreating the style of the painter she's modelled herself on, that she can produce infinite variations on his themes, as the painter himself never did ... yet it still looks like Van Gogh. The issue we're confronting is the old Homeric one: the author is plural, constituted through tradition.

In Homeric tradition, the narrator's honesty is manifested through respect for the canonical nesting of the scenes and actions that constitute the narrative framework, itself repeatedly rearranged through oral improvisation (Lord, 1965). We researchers of the density and true quality of the real, are we modern-day bards, fashioning the epic deeds of scholarly adventurers in our revues? Charged with the mission of communication, our task would be to communicate the experiences of others by disentangling their plots ... Would this make us others' authors, in a Bakhtinian sense, but with affiliations to Ricoeur? Phenomenologists of others' perceptions, would this make us the symbolizing fiction makers of the motivations for teaching?

I'm coming back down to earth. Soon the video of *Vincent and Me* will be over. The heroine found the forger in Amsterdam, and thanks to her he's been caught. The journalist whom the young painter's father assigned to guide her has taken the credit for the forger's capture. She learns of the false claim when she turns on the television. I'm floating on the canals of Amsterdam with the heroine of the movie. This August I'll be attending a conference there. All I know of Holland comes from its writers and some email. The film is over. I'm at the back of a class of twenty-five pupils. Little by little, the children have come closer to the television monitor; with small stealthy movements, their bodies slumped on tables, they've formed a compact mass, like a raft being gently tossed by a light swell. A gentle atmosphere has filled the classroom. When, abruptly, the light comes on, all the bodies straighten up.

Leaving this rural school, I'm still soaked in the atmosphere of unity created by the story we all lived through together. As I go back into town, the sun beats down on the car I rented for the occasion, and I switch on the air conditioning. I travelled 2,000 miles to meet these teachers, but the difference between the worlds of Manitoba's and Quebec's schools – or even Switzerland's schools, for I encountered similar readings and concerns *(Diana's Runaway*, Anne Frank's *Diary of a Young Girl)* – is less than the gulf between the epistemologies of the two classes I observed this morning, with only a wall between them.

Do these teachers talk to each other? This leads me reflect on the academic world as well. Sometimes contact is so easy with colleagues from other universities. The differentness of neighbours requires us to make a mental effort. Thus there is a point of contact between the realities experienced by teachers at different levels. But how could this teacher ever have a sense of the lives of educator-researchers, who are responsible for building meaning across nations? Paradoxically, our timetables limit us little, yet we're under great time and space constraints, as we continent-hop in order to communicate points of view.

I was to come back from Amsterdam with little ceramic houses, whose image I've just encountered in Soja's *Thirdspace* (1996, p. 284). As McLaren (1998, p. xiv) has written, 'our desires are shaped by the semiotic network within subjects articulating their subjective positions.' Individuals may be close to each other geographically and yet not cooperate with each other because they do not belong to the same conceptual beam. This was true of the two teachers above: their epistemic spaces were not shared.

Case 4

The academic world is an intersection of conceptual and physical geographies. In the following journal entry the geography of the class is imbued with the spirit of an Elizabethan play and becomes the locus of the drama. The teacher embodies the main character and prompts the attainment of historical awareness among the students by spatializing information through action and gesture. He makes history synchronic in a closed space in order to better transmit the acting mind of the play.

The carving up of space into semiotic beams is well illustrated by the centrifugal labyrinth that is Amsterdam, whose levels and islets embody various social segments – some of which are at the heart of the city's reputation.

Research Journal – 14 May 1993

Before we went into class, this teacher told me that he knew exactly how the lesson will go and that his planning is worked out down to the word. He outlined his plan to me and then lowered the blinds, partly to create an atmosphere and partly so the transparencies will be easier to read. He's been teaching high school for twenty-six years. He's given this lesson twenty-six times and improved it each year, to the point where it's almost a theatrical performance.

The students arrive. The teacher talks very softly. He's summarizing *Macbeth*. His voice becomes full and rich, and bit by bit he reveals transparencies that have faded over the years. Later, after the lesson, he will explain to me that his improvement for next year will be to redo the transparencies in two colours, red and blue, and in capital letters. The students listen to him with bated breath. A fine public speaker, he plunges us into the universe of Elizabethan beliefs where light represented good and darkness evil. What are we doing in the darkness of this classroom? The light comes from transparencies, illuminating the class with codified knowledge. The objects are invisible but they have been clothed in colour.

When attention flags, the teacher raises his voice, walks among the tables, makes striking gestures, asks a question, ties the play in with life experiences, suggesting obscure connections. Suddenly, he wakes the students up by comparing Macbeth's powers to those of rock singers. It's a dicey comparison, the court of a Scottish king with rock groupies, but the teacher's speech grows animated and his words flow in an access of contained excitement. For a moment, in the darkness, the students are bewitched. 'I' figures ever more prominently among his pronouns, as the talk grows personal. 'I am Macbeth'; the teacher strikes his own breast. 'How shall I control my nobles when the invader is about to strike? These noblemen can't change their colours too soon, it would endanger them; so I have time to bring them together in my castle. There I'll shut them in and I'll have discretionary power ...' Every anecdote is measured and part of the plan. The teacher takes out a coin and makes it jump on the back of his hand. He calls up the witches, the two sides of life. Macbeth thought he was invincible; he failed to understand the depth of the signs.

After the lesson, the teacher will explain to me how hard it is for seventeen-year-old students to grasp the plot. Since they no longer read, you have to predigest the work for them. Over twenty-six years, little by little, this teacher has condensed the structural information in *his* lesson, but at the same time he's been careful to flesh it out with anecdotes that are close to their day-to-day lives. Moreover, this lesson has become an exemplum of his personal research on Elizabethan symbolism. He has become fused with his own lesson, making it into a model for living, a staging of his deepest philosophy, a lesson in ethics, in complicity with the play's great narrative moves.

Still stunned by this display, I am helping him raise the blinds to let light in for the students again. The blind rolls up badly. I tug impatiently at the blind. I wreck the blind. As I leave the classroom after the interview, this teacher observes, with seemingly concealed pity, 'That was a successful lesson, apart from my blind that you wrecked.' And, as I walk away somewhat embarrassed, I hear him as he gets out a stapler: 'I'm used to it, it's been happening to me for twenty-six years.'

An echo of this situation can be found in Stanton Wortham's research, as described in *Acting out Participant Examples in the Classroom* (1994). Wortham notes that in classrooms that follow the philosophy of *paideia*, students and teachers act out social texts. The literary text 'provides an implicit script for the classroom interaction itself' (p. vi). 'Unwittingly, they adopt the roles described in texts under study and enact the issues, among themselves' (p. v). Through deictic mapping, Wortham reconstructs their spaces of interaction, how the classroom geography maps out the geography of the text: 'The students, being members of an underprivileged social group, clearly identify with their subordinate counterparts in the text' (ibid.). They act out their roles 'while the teachers – themselves members of a higher status group – play the role of the powerful and dominate them' (ibid.).

Reasserting a Spatialized Ontology

In this chapter, I have said that two ways of approaching spatial conceptualization have been dominant historically. One is top-down and Avicennian; it leads to a view of manifestations and their geography as the breaking through of an integrative meaning (creation being indissociable from the creation of meaning). This integrative meaning is manifested in meaning families, in the form of meaning beams that bring together 'epistemes' using signs that imply the correspondence, or congruence, between mind and matter. This congruence is achieved through the agent intellect – the acting mind. The acting mind is the integrative link between unmanifested meaning and its manifestation. Thanks to the acting mind, space takes on meaning. This conception of space, although referring to origins as the focal site of knowledge, remains ahistorical in principle. A second ahistorical conception was proposed by Edward Soja during the 1980s and further developed in his 1996 book. Based on the data of urban geography, this conception, taking a post-Marxist, metacritical perspective, proposes to valorize spatiality by showing how much geography predetermines both individual and collective action. For example, geographical proximity privileges certain populations, as in the example of Kenya cited above, and certain social classes occupy a dominant geography. This bottom-up version of the emergence of spatial sense is, *a priori*, physical and materialist.

The cases I have cited suggest that in certain educational contexts the Avicennian acting mind would seem to explain the power of metaphor to model space by affecting the spatialization of meaning that is the acting mind's subproduct. In this light, I am inclined to propose a neo-Avicennian description of spatiality, in the sense that meaning prevails over contingency. The two conceptions, however, may differ because of a simple difference of perspective that could be reconciled within a third perspective. Geography, after all, is under the control of a three- dimensional universe. In four-dimensional space-time, past, present, and future disappear, yielding fully to the redimensionality envisioned by both Avicenna and Edward Soja. History is born of the order imposed upon phenomena by the observer. It is possible to conceive that the lines of individual cohesion would be different in a different dimensionality. This would enable the emergence from an absolute temporal perspective. Becoming relative, time would become regional: it would depend on geographical points of view. A relativist present would design the elsewhere, the omega, for each observer.

Edward Soja's conceptions are politically correct and useful, but no less circumscribed, for all that, by a classical mechanics whose geometry is limited to the domain of the perceptible by the community that shares a given meaning beam. It is realistic to suppose that reflection on other possible dimensionalities would relativize this ontology. For example,

reflection would show that spatio-temporal consciousness is wholly circumscribed neither by material forms nor by semiotic models, but rather
that their joint actualization gives birth, within the substance of conceptual relations, to meanings in process of becoming, meanings that give
energetic nutriment to, and are necessary for the maintenance of, the
acting mind.

In discussing the primacy of history or geography, we should not
forget that time and space intersect. Many symbolic systems articulate
space and time, and they do not always conceive of the intersection to
the detriment of space. As an example, I would like to offer the narratives that accompany *dhulaŋs*, the animal map-histories found in Aus-
tralia. The story of a crocodile and its postures presents geographic
locations so specifically that one can refer to it for the purposes of travel.
Topographical knowledge may be transmitted through myth: 'The *dhulaŋ*
represents a specific place where the crocodile (an Ancestral Being)
lives, and the graphic elements are organised on spatial principles: that
is, they are intended to correspond to elements of the landscape. Hence
it is a map. However, it is obviously a highly conventional map. In order
to be able to read it, you have to know something of the stories, songs
and dances of the creation of this landscape by this Ancestral Being and
his kin' (Turnbull, 1993, p. 33). Thus, even the land of the Ancients, its
intimate geography, corresponds to a mythic narrative that is transmitted from generation to generation of the Gumatj people to delimit their
territory. In this chapter I believe I have supported the hypothesis that
an image can constitute the expression of the acting mind, an expression
cast before space and before time, a form that alludes to the elsewhere, to
possible complicity, to creative complicity.

New York and Los Angeles are poles in the mythic space of urban
education. Seeking inspiration while I was rereading and rewriting this
text, I rented two videos: Wim Wenders's *Wings of Desire* – he learned his
art in New York – and its American remake *City of Angels,* starring
Nicholas Cage and Meg Ryan. Standing outside time, the angels of
Berlin people the space of Los Angeles, like impassive vultures ready to
swoop down on ordinary people. They stand everywhere, atop buildings
and on the beach, and have a totalizing vision, but can only come into
true existence if they fall, if they pass to action by taking on a body that
bleeds and suffers. 'O God! I could be bounded in a nutshell, and count
myself a king of infinite space,' quotes Soja from *Hamlet* (II, 2) in his
1989 'Afterwords.' And, like the angels in *City of Angels,* Edward Soja
contemplates the city in its multiple aspects, listening to the voices of

human beings declare their existence in the immobility of time: 'I have been looking at Los Angeles from many different points of view and each way of seeing assists in sorting out the interjacent medley of the subject landscape. The perspectives explored are purposeful, eclectic, fragmentary, incomplete, and frequently contradictory, but so too is Los Angeles and, indeed, the experienced historical geography of every urban landscape. Totalizing visions, attractive though they may be, can never capture all the meanings and significations of the urban.' (Soja, 1989, p. 247).

CHAPTER FIVE

A Manifesto for Didaction: Action Poetry as an Empowering Myth

Like the previous chapters, the present manifesto attempts to find one possible junction between culture, thought, and action. Action can have an educational dimension. In this sense, didaction would be a characteristic move of the acting mind.

A postmodern position would have it that the border between science and art is fuzzy. Both rest on a set of paradigmatic connections that emerge from shared practices. Both are communitarian practices based on convictions inherent in the establishment of rules and local values. In short, both scientific and artistic culture emerge from historicized actions and thus, necessarily, from literature. The postmodern attitude defines a way of thinking and a methodology related to the superstructures of knowledge and action. Its underlying framework, which contradicts the traditional sense of objectivity, eliminates the idea of a single and best way. The resulting ontological uncertainty leaves the social actor searching for new ways of expression. Postmodern selfhood articulates itself in the quest for a new shared meaning and metacommunication in a reflective community. Following the line suggested by Bachelard in 1932, selfhood is fully realized only in the immediate instant, *hic et nunc.* Thus the postmodern identity appears always contingent and is linked to the realization of ephemera.

According to this contemporary conception of things, cultures spring from the linguistic and communicative specificities proper to various fields of action. These fields of action correspond to expressive paradigms suited to the construction of specific cultural values. In this respect, postmodernism reconciles literature and action, whereas the contextual dimension of literary action partly eluded structuralism. The present chapter employs the essay mode to explore the transposition from social action to original creation made possible through specific poetic performances, despite, and indeed within, the frame of reference of the school. I analyse the didactic implications of the poetic transposition into action and the construction of a possible ethics of a postmodern, empowering action literature by means of the poetic sign.

Through several narratives of experience, I will present lived processes of poetic emergence in French-speaking Switzerland and francophone Northern Ontario. These processes suggest the benefits of transcending the usual structural options in instruction on the literary art object, given the integrative possibilities of action and of poetic action in particular. In order to integrate the dynamics of creation, didactics in schools could work from active, post-structuralist principles and become 'didactive,' that is, pedagogically active along a trend that defines learning as the creation of entirely new knowledge, concepts, and artefacts.

School Genres and Didaction

The international educational trend called *didactics* appears to be almost unknown in the English-speaking world, although it constitutes a major movement in many non-English-speaking countries. Simply put, didactics is the study of meaning-making processes in one specific subject matter or discipline. It would, however, be reductive to assimilate didactics with curriculum and instruction at large: it studies the particular relationships that exist and are actualized between the three poles of the didactic triangle composed of the learner, the teacher, and the disciplinary subject matter. Research into, and the practice of, didactics are based on the premise that we can construct a pedagogy for each subject matter taught: a didactics of language, a didactics of mathematics, a didactics of the arts, and so on. Didactics emphasizes the singularity of each teaching situation and attempts to integrate academic content with current theories of education and pedagogy (Bertrand & Houssaye, 1999). The assumption is that the relationship to knowledge is different in each discipline, and is specific to particular objects of knowledge. For instance, the relationship that fifth-grade students may have with a particular mathematical topic can be very different from that they may have with learning to paint a portrait, and each learning relationship presents different pedagogical problems. Each specific type of knowledge should have its specific pedagogy. You cannot teach a classical language such as Latin like any modern language: the emphasis is not conversational in

Latin, and the oral exchange does not have the same value, and so on for each discipline. In a sense, didactics is the study of the disciplinary, pedagogical differences that are the most useful to teachers. Didactics is a lively field of research in many countries, and any old-fashioned associations that may cling to the English word *didactic* should be dismissed in connection with this field (Tochon, 1999a).

This chapter will show how creation and action may transcend subject-matter planning. Indeed, it is inherently paradoxical to try to plan authentic creation (Tochon, 2000b). The notion of authentic action and creation in a classroom setting may be presumptuous: how can one prepare for situations that will promote authenticity? Ways of producing authenticity in a school setting remain mysterious, and the creative arts are taught in a classroom setting that is usually less than authentic. There are indications of communicative authenticity in children's behaviour, but it is not clear that this serves school goals. Thus there is a gap between authentic creation or action as planned for the classroom, and authentic creation or action as experienced in real life, even within the artificial context of the school.

Herewith, then, a proposal for *didaction,* a new kind of instructional action: not top-down and planning-oriented, but bottom-up and based in lived actualization. Four characteristics of didaction are as follows:

1 Didaction proceeds from the natural flow of a personal initiative occurring within a frame that fosters autonomous individual action and the follow-up to its achievement (Csikszentmihalyi & Csikszentmihalyi, 1988).
2 Didaction sets up the value of life as action and thus assumes a political, meaningful, and creative dimension.
3 Didaction rests on a consensual, flexible ethics adapted to the creative context.
4 Didactive appraisal progresses as action unfolds and in relation with the progressive clarity of representation of the goal.

Experiences from French-Speaking Switzerland

Postmodernism has granted biographic writing a whole new form of legitimacy. In this spirit I will here present how certain aesthetic reflections led me to conceive of action poetry from 1982 to 1986 in the French-speaking region of Switzerland, known as *la Suisse romande.* Action poetry is poetry put into action, a kind of poetic action-research that intends to change social life in a poetic way. As poetics relate to meaning-making processes, action poetry can be framed into didaction, an action that is aimed to change society in an educational way. This narrative of experience suggests a break between a didactics of the poetic object within a structuralist frame of reference and lived action flowing from the poem.[1] Actually, when poetry becomes action, the poetic act is more than an ephemeral urban decor: it becomes – etymologically speaking – a political call.

Papering the City with Poems

As an active member of Geneva's authors' society, I was grieved by the disappearance of poetry from urban life (Roth, 1983; Sola, 1987). Poetry interested few people; publishers of poetry barely survived. After all, who had the time to read poetry? It was thus that I conceived the idea of papering the city with poems. The cities of Geneva and Vernier allocated money for the posting of seventy-seven poems on public billboards in March and April 1985 (Tochon, 1985b). Every poem was inscribed by hand on an original background created in acrylics by the painter Mireille Wagnière (except for ten backgrounds done by the graphic artist Helen Tilbury). This was evanescent artwork: after one month, the poems were covered over with advertising. Nevertheless, this exercise in action poetry triggered a rash of articles in daily newspapers and magazines (Martin, 1985a; Matter, 1985) and radio and television programs.

In the same spirit, the billboard company allotted a huge downtown space for the posting of a poem for peace for two months. The poem was inscribed upon a background featuring an acrylic collage by painters Denise Rauss and Isabelle Lebeau. This was recognized by the Guinness book of records for Europe as the largest poem in the world. Because it was placed on metal panels that the billboard company needed to recover afterwards, the poem was destroyed after being exhibited.

Students in Action Poetry

The initiative did not pass unnoticed by students, who enlarged on it themselves. They created poems to musical backgrounds, some of which were recorded in studio; and they painted poem posters, several of which were put up in town. A poem by a student named Séverine Michellod was posted in the Old City and attracted the attention of a journalist who dedicated a whole page to the subject in a local weekly. A year later, Geneva poet Huguette Junod launched another initiative deriving from this whole experience. Since then, giant poems on bill-boards have turned up from time to time.

In action poetry, performance produces a metaphoric message, which may take a narrative dimension. Action, which before all else is abstract, erects a set of values into a series of metaphoric symbols. These values cannot be separated from the context and the field of action, and yet they present the poetic sign as a means of reaching beyond the symbolic connections usually promoted by the city. Through poetry, the city appears to be refigured – as Paul Ricoeur (1984) would put it – and rejuvenated.

The Act of the Heart

During this time, metamorphosis had been felt as a transcendence of structuralism and of structuralist fixity. The wave of poems in 1984–5 aimed first and foremost to convey a sense of poetry as urban essence or urban psyche, but the very material nature of the sign transformed into action caused this process to evolve; action was the bearer of poetry, and poetry seemed to be the sole goal, sufficient unto itself as it emerged as a value revealed to the world. Although this poetry touched the city, at the outset politics were almost wholly absent from it, as though the necessary transformation must be internal, and any expression besides change itself were undesirable. In reality, however, the poetry intrinsic in the presentation of its own signs was becoming political, almost, one might say, *etymologically*, from the moment it penetrated urban life. How could billboard poems be free of ideology? Their ideology, which was the bearer of emotion, was located in the affirmation of poetry, love, and peace. In a development of the first project, this same emotion led me to inscribe poems on watercolours and then, by means of several slides, impose fragments of art on giant screens and deconstruct them a single beat after.

Action poetry was intent, then, on freeing itself from the dichotomies that restrict the arts; it was synaesthetic and brought liberated analogies to bear on lived experience. In the classroom, the passage from action poetry to action research allowed for osmosis among students and my-self. The students realized the importance of knowledge in action. This approach ceased to be overly sanitized, or inauthentic, as soon as students saw in it the opportunity to raise their voices for the sake of a cause. The cause motivated them, because without it, no true problems appeared to stir their hearts in daily life. The Wittgensteinian poetic play of ideas suddenly acquired the urgency of a fight for survival.

The gesture called the Act of the Heart emerged from an initiative of mine in 1985. It consisted of a group dedicated to collaborative self-training in action poetry. Our goal was to organize a large-scale poetic action that was to be non-denominational, non-political, and not-for-profit. We wished to stimulate thought towards the ecological. Through the Act of the Heart, action poetry acquired an educational dimension: poetry became social action(Martin, 1985b). Whatever our declared intentions, the Act of the Heart led to the emergent politicization of the literary, to *literaction*. Declared apoliticism more truly bespoke a will to contribute to a different politics, a politics of the other that would be humanist and not reductive to oppositions of right and left (Morin, 1967).

'Life-Lines': An Action Poem for Life

The action poem 'L'Agir du Coeur' (translated as 'Life-Lines' in English) was conceived as a prayer without religion. The goal was to spread conceptual energy in a collectively useful direction by the declaration of common objectives for survival: 'To love, because present-day spiritual anaemia appears to be coupled with emotional famine; to act, because action in thought alone is not sufficient for change.' Loving and acting were to be applied to peace, to food shortages and poverty, and to' major ecological problems: pollution of the soil, air, and water. The poem would have love pass to action and burn through problems.

This action poem was distributed from Geneva on 12 December 1985. Fifty thousand postcards were printed with the poem and instructions to send the poem to friends abroad so that it would spread as fast as possible, and to think about the poem for several months. A press conference was organized to launch the action poem and to put forward the idea of a tax to benefit the Third·World. The poem was translated into eighteen languages and distributed in some forty countries. For several months, thousands of people thought about a poem for life.

LIFE-LINES: AN ACTION POEM FOR LIFE

Pure light
We are many who love
We love for peace
We love so that all may eat

We love so that the earth may be pure
We love so that our water may be pure
We love so that our air may be pure
We love so that a space of love
Will build up among all human beings

Let the fire of love
Burn all our problems with love

Pure light

We are many to act
We act for peace
We act so that all may eat
We act so that the earth may be pure
We act so that our water may be pure
We act so that our air may be pure
We act so that a force of love
Will build up in human beings

Let the fire of love
Burn all our problems with love

Other Francophone Experiences

In a similar vein, I'd like to present experiences of action poetry by a
Franco-Ontarian poet born in Ottawa, Jean-Marc Dalpé. (Jacqueline
Dumas introduced me to his work; Tochon, 1994.) Dalpé's poetry is put
into action through his theatre; his theme is linguistic survival. The
actor-poet lives where two genres intersect: the linearity of drama, occurring in sequential time, and the rupture of poetry, occurring in atemporal
paradigms. Dalpé's writing and speech translate a situation of linguistic
rupture: rupture between English and French (*Romeo and Juliet* is bilingual), between the rich and the poor, between elevated and popular
language, and between generations. Dalpé conceives of poetry as a
gesture made towards purity (but not towards purism, which is why he
rejects elitism). Like other Northern Ontario poets (Patrice Desbiens,
Michel Vallières, Michel Gallaire), Dalpé offers powerful, disturbing
poetry rooted in claims for both linguistic and political existence (Dumas,
1990). He is highly regarded by young people and undertakes tours of
high schools. His utterances are thus reinvested in the teaching of

French and serve as the foundation for interdiscursive action. His poetry shows a blend of rhythm, sound, and meaning, and revive a particular history 'in order to never be silent again' (Fugère, 1989; Tassé, 1990). Inspired by his work, classes write and present sketches and restore the dimension of sound to the Word. Students organize performances and enter into action poetry.

Dalpé has attained some prominence thanks to the TNO (Theatre Northern Ontario) in Sudbury. His pieces, including *Shouts and Blues, Romeo and Juliet* and, especially, *Dogs,* have met with considerable success. Some 2,500 spectators saw *Dogs* in the Franco-Ontarian Théâtre-Action, while the English-language version staged in Toronto drew 2,700 spectators. Dalpé's poetry collections display the same performative force of expression: *Les murs de nos villages* (The walls of our villages, 1983), *Ceux d'ici* (Those who come from here, 1984a), and *Et d'ailleurs* (And from elsewhere, 1984b). 'Don't be afraid of busting your face / as long as you open your mouth / Our whole history is one of broken open mouths / and, too often, also / silent broken mouths' (Dalpé, 1983, translation by Rina Kampeas).

The actor-poet, the 'labourer of speech,' has lost his homeland but found his identity through language ('We had our language in our pockets / but our pockets had holes in them,' ibid.) and in the effort of sawing through the chains that inhibit free expression.

>Si on avait le coeur de dire
>toutes ces chaînes qui nous retiennent
>Si on avait des yeux de dire
>tous ces soleils qu'on nous voile
>Si on avait les mains de dire
>tous ces coups qui nous tombent dessus
>Si on avait les pieds de dire
>tous ces chemins de travers
>qu'on nous invite à prendre
>Si on avait le ventre de dire
>toute cette musique qu'on nous interdit
>Si on avait la langue de dire
>tous ces mots qui sont menottés au silence
>
>(If we had the heart to speak
>all the chains that hold us back
>If we had the eyes to speak
>all the suns that are veiled to us

If we had the hands to speak
all the blows that rain on us
If we had the feet to speak
all the wrong roads
we are urged to take
If we had the guts to speak
all the music we are forbidden
If we had the tongue to speak
all these words handcuffed to silence)

                              (Dalpé, 1983, p. 39, translation by Rina Kampeas)[2]

For Dalpé, poetry is action: it saws through bars and handcuffs and frees one from slavery by giving voice to the oppressed aspects of one's being:

Il y a des barreaux aux fenêtres de chaque coeur d'homme.
On les forge de fer et d'ignorance
On les pose de force en douce
La poésie est une scie.

(There are bars in the windows of every human heart.
They are forged from iron and indifference
They are gently installed by force
Poetry is a saw.)

                              (Dalpé, 1983, p. 20, translation by Rina Kampeas)

One last example of action poetry: the poetry workshop for *griots* (Amoa, 1994). The griot is a musician-poet who has a lot of prestige in traditional African society. In the West Indies, griots organize poetry workshops to assemble the villages around common political goals. The action poetry of griots has emerged from a dual activism. Each evening the griot seduces the child with the magic of words (Fitte-Duval, 1992, p. 30). Griots are poets, musicians, and historians of the community in the Caribbean islands; their action is educational, identity-building, and combats the insecurity of diglossia. The evening of the griot, a political microculture, is built from moment to moment in tune with every participant and resists assimilation. This is poetry as a different action.

The Politicization of the Teacher

The opening of this chapter suggests examples of action poetry, of an action through which poetry could become cross-artistic and promote a politics of the othernessing of values. In French-speaking Switzerland and Northern Ontario, action poetry touched students' lives: billboard poems opened up avenues for creation in the classroom and the actor-poet promoted a local cultural expression in schools. In both cases, action is educational and yet not didactic. These actions rest on a creative principle. Is this principle transferable to didactics? If so, which didactics? The didactics of world languages will be examined below from a postmodern perspective.

Poetic space rests on the effulgence of meaning in a time freed from all constraints other than reflection on the sign. Free time, open space: is this the definition of the classroom? The classroom is a space with a certain minimal closure, aiming towards the transmission of formalized epistemologies. At its heart, a class is a group entity governed by standards. Even if these standards are not imposed by the teacher or the institution, they emerge implicitly from the group. Conceptually, the class-group is a minimal paradigm, a field for action governed by local epistemologies as well as more general ways of thinking. As such, it metamorphoses through the interactions that occur within it as a conceptual unity, creating a microculture in the process of change (and sometimes of evolution).

One problem of creative action is that it is unforeseeable. If literature is to be inserted into this microcultural space-time of the group, it can be integrated by top-down means (prefabricated conceptual spaces are then integrated into the surrounding microculture) or by bottom-up means (the meaning is grasped by individuals who share it with the group, and the group fixes the meaning in a consensual space-time that sometimes emerges into action). Mixed methods may be used, following principles of alternation or embedding. For some years now, curriculum designers have been stymied in disseminating their models by the difficulty of foreseeing both the process and the product of creation. Full foresight necessitates top-down prefabrication, which often inhibits the creation of the new. Thus neither content nor its form can be wholly foreseeable. The solution is to create a consensual space within which individual expression is permitted. Keeping in mind the teacher-content-learner triangle (Houssaye, 1994), the *angles* of the didactic triangle must be differentiated from the relational *arrows* that represent the dynamics that operate within it. The structure of the triangle constitutes a given *state* of the relationship and conceptually fixes specific, idiosyncratic pedagogical dynamics. In this perspective, true interaction exceeds the frame of didactic foreseeability: conceptual interaction entails dynamics that cannot be foreseen, and even reverse dynamics, which can generate the emergence of a counterculture unforeseen by the teacher. Thus, McDermott (1976) and Buckley and Cooper (1978) have shown how, in class, children develop strategies to *not* learn. One can even imagine the existence of a *counterinstruction*, a possible product of Jackson's (1968) implicit 'nil curriculum.' The countercultural role of creation has been the subject of discussion since the early period of postmodernist thought: there is no need to insist on it here.

Epistemological reflection on the nature of anticipation suggests the difficulty of foreseeing the bottom-up processes of creation in an instructional framework. Top-down processes can be foreseen, because they flow from pre-established consensual standards. Bottom-up processes are born of momentary consensus that emerge from the situation. For example, a counterculture in process of being ratified and standardized is an emergent political phenomenon specific to a field of action that cannot be reduced to dominant conceptual paradigms. Initially, its process is bottom-up. On the other hand, action poetry appears to emerge from a mixed process, because it incorporates some aspects of consensus in order to manifest itself. Would it be possible, then, to make its consensual aspects valid for instruction?

Since didactics are defined in terms of generalizable anticipation, they rest on consensual elements. To be integrated into didactics, action poetry would have to be articulated around a definitional consensus that would allow for the generalization of this type of action. Now, although action poetry is political in its representation of a conceptual minority, and, indeed, rests on minimal consensus, it also must incorporate bottom-up processes of formation and consist of original (nonconsensual) components. The consensual, nonoriginal elements of action poetry that can be articulated in didactics are the category-specific and paradigmatic elements that transpose, not lived experience, but representational features that authorize poetic expression. In practice, the problem is that curriculum designers can never be certain that, in lived experience, their category-specific scaffolding will result in the intended effects. What may just be possible is that a didactic design not built on the anticipatory organization of contents, but rather on its motivational relations to the infinite possibilities of creation, could be redeveloped into personal strategies.

At the Junction of Education and Politics

The conceptual organizers specific to didactics, then, must simultaneously play the role of motivational organizers, by establishing links with students' lived experience. What is needed are indexical links. If didactic organizers are subject to the terms of a life action taken on as a personal project (Tochon, 1990b), they become didactive. Didaction is thus located at the junction of the didactic and the pedagogical. It takes account of pedagogical variability and bases itself on creative, motivational elements that emerge from interactions.

The perspective of classical didactics is to develop a set of cognitive goals with a view to mastering the conceptual and assessable aspects of linguistic production. The *didactive* perspective, on the other hand, proceeds from a whole different concern. Working from the post-structuralist principle according to which every methodology is ideological (Galisson, 1985), it seeks to elicit the organization of linguistic action by motivating the individual to express his or her personal voice, to assume a political responsibility for change, and to do these things autonomously, with no process of appraisal beyond that of satisfying the communicative goal. Thus the individual assumes his or her own ideology and, in a sense, expresses his or her microculture. The individual is empowered to speak. In this perspective, action is organized in an organic fashion and didactic organizers properly so called, those of the curriculum, develop on the basis of the action that unfolds.

In an analysis of the 'authorized' expressions of the student Séverine Michellod (namely, her urban billboard) and those of Dalpé's fans (rock-poetry school performances), it will be observed that, irrespective of the instructional guidelines, in the structural sense of the term, the expressive gesture is itself the bearer of a sufficiently flagrant meaning for action to flow from it self-motivated. Idea is tied in with the various logics of action. Ideology, functioning as an engine, implies methodology; working from initial personal creative impulses, the teacher indexes those organizational elements of the curriculum that are the most favourable to the development of knowledge in action. Examples like these lead one to reflect on the place of the school and the choices that have led to the purging of the faintest move towards the political from school-based actions. It's true that the inherent danger of explicit politics, its anti-educational potential, is doctrinal manipulation. But measures can be taken to preserve autonomous decision making and the expression of personal ideas through the choice of different possible actions and their methods of implementation. As has already been said, the politicization of constructive values – survival values – in a school context can be linked to a politics of the human that transcends concepts of right and left. It can be matched to a taxonomy of commitment through autonomous action. Although the taxonomy of affective goals devised by Krathwohl, Bloom, and Masia (1964) has proven dangerous when ideal goals are imposed on it, nevertheless the potential for harm in constructivist social involvement is reduced if the choice of positive action is left to the individual; in this manner didaction can be extended to the arts, to science, to social and philanthropic work, to environmentalism.

Literaction as Social Intervention

Consideration of the classroom situation from a didactive perspective requires a change in the ways we conceptualize intervention. Classically, intervention has been organized by a syntax. This syntactic perspective has prevailed in the formalization of certain didactic models whose structuralist dimension cannot be denied. In didactics, the context of intervention is understood as entailing a category-based division that allows one to proceed in stages. The rationale of didactics rests on the generalization of a set of instructional procedures: principles of intervention are decontextualized so that they can be transferred to potential new situations. In contrast, didactics emerges not from a morphosyntax of generalized action, but rather from differential semantic elements subject to being actualized in individual pragmatic ways. Didaction is situated in the search for the most significant fields of action from the perspective of the microculture that emerges when 'personal projects' are brought together with an educational goal. School curricula form conceptual fields that are adjusted after the fact to the cultural and political initiatives that are most likely to attract autonomous conceptual energies with a potential to be positively creative.

In the field of arts and aesthetics, *literaction* is a particular field in which literary and cultural action meld. This field is socially didactive, being aimed at social intervention. Action poetry occurs within literaction, and literaction is not fully foreseeable. To some extent it slips out from under the didactic framework. Quite possibly it has a historic dimension that allows for post hoc detection of an introduction, a trigger event, a transformation, a development, and a conclusion; but all these emerge from a reconstitution. Didaction is cathartic and, within school-authorized zones, it produces the elements that lead to organizational rupture, allowing individuals to understand that a legitimate part of their own motivation to live and express themselves can be made concrete in the here and now.

Thus, didaction is based as much on conceptual organizers indexed to the enacted curriculum as it is on disorganizers that have been polarized by the proximal zone of the freedom to learn, conceive, and create. These didactic disorganizers have been presented in a corpus of verbalizations, by thirty experienced language teachers, of lesson plans (Tochon, 1991). The instructional disorganizer is an abstract element whose connection with task domains or work spaces must be created by the learner himself or herself. The disorganizer is a 'problem poser' that prompts didactic suspension. It is an element from which it is neither certain nor required that the following element will be reached. Disorganizers prompt both activation and transcendence of the didactic.

Contents are of interest to didaction only to the extent that they propel individual energies towards the building of a socially constructivist identity. Deconstruction of the paradoxes and contradictions inherent in the planned action consists of an introspective move that supplements the stage of creative development. The intentionality that underlies the poem is alternately laid bare and then 'enacted' through a becoming that is individual, then shared, and thus political. The contradictions of becoming are resolved in the creative action. The strategies developed thus become individual and situational and correspond to only partial predetermination.

Appraisal in Creative Education

School-based necessity entails appraisal of actions and their results. Once the goal becomes didactive and no longer corresponds to the necessary preliminary, but rather to the necessary aftermath, what becomes of assessment? Well, nothing prevents the devising of a didactic contract (or consensus) as things unfold, which would set objectives for a project in process of being conducted. If the formula then proved to limit action excessively by making the venues for creativity too rigid, the contract or consensus could be based, not on objectives, but on *proximal challenges*, determined from situation to situation, as creation progressed. Challenges could be negotiated in order to index them to curricular items. Thus consensual components would underlie the original components of action. In a framework of this kind, the communication of assessment would come down to decoding its language.

But an epistemological reflection must nevertheless be conducted on the postmodern dimensions of assessment. For this purpose I am taking

as a point of departure Louis-Marie Ouellette's analysis (1996) of interactive assessment. In the tradition of Bateson, Castoriadis, and Serre,
Ouellette shows the role of communication (that is, of context and
culture) in formative assessment, given its essentially interactive aspect.
According to Ouellette, the dynamics of knowledge are translated into
the variation in transformations perceived in a bounded universe. These
transformations affect either the immediate or the long term. Assessment can isolate elements for reflection elicited by observation and
transfer them to a level where they can be articulated into virtual models
of responses. This process transforms immediate experience into a message about reality. The assessment proceeds to perform operations on
knowledge by developing descriptive propositions about factual history
and the direction it tends towards. Reflection for assessment purposes
thus exceeds individual boundaries by entailing constant interaction
between the transformative period of existence of representations of the
real, and the space that moulds them in line with local characteristics.

In this process, knowledge bears its own standard, that standard being
the elicitation of the aim of the process. Assessment is experienced
through statements describing perceptions in line with elicitations linked
to the context in which the experience unfolds (Ouellette, 1996). Assessment of this kind comes close to being research; such research is an
expression of individual responsibility. By expressing his or her position
in relation to the real, the individual articulates his or her representation
of the real. Once conceptualized through the process of assessment, the
real no longer exists only in the self. It resides in the relation between
the individual and a collectivity, a movement of thought. Assessment of
an object, by virtue of the fact that the observer is unavoidably situated in
a field of observation, therefore translates an unlimited succession of
relationships.

If this postmodern conception of assessment is integrated into
didaction, didactive assessment will then transform the object into a
relationship and subject the discrete reality of the object to question.
Through its very relationship with its reality, the object is transformed
and undergoes a variation that corresponds to the search for meaning.
By identifying his or her position on a trajectory, the creator who observes his or her creation is involved in a whole whose internal consistency communicates local knowledge. This local microculture is nourished
by the representation of relations with the object, to the extent that it
reflects an organized image of the object and its development. Contents

specific to the object flow from (as opposed to following upon) successive approximations and reconstructions of the object, in the sense that they explicate reality and motivate the creative trajectory.

The cohesiveness of the creative context, then, no longer depends on a taxonomy of goals, but rather on an elucidation of the representations that motivate action. At the same time, these motives for action rise up as standards, in the sense that the standard can no longer be separated from the explicit explanation of action. Henceforward, the opposition between criterion-based and standard-based references in assessment has no reason for existence. Standards proceed from successive adjustments of relations between the individual and the conceptual consistency he or she is constructing, deconstructing, and reconstructing, in the ceaselessly renewed search for a fit with the representation of the object of his or her action.

Creation as the Locus of *Différance*

In this chapter, I have defined the didactive perspective as postmodern. It situates aesthetic education in the autonomous possibility of constructive emergence from the relation with others. In its artistic and discursive expressions, this connection is creative. It is partially planned but it eludes the representational exhaustiveness upon customary school evaluations rest. Evaluation becomes a didactive appraisal. Appraisal is the product and the process of creation or action, rather than its criterion-based anticipation. This position leads to a denunciation of the myth according to which it is possible to plan the representational course of others' learning. In contrast to this myth, didaction is a personal affair; it does not differ from the motivational possibilities of the individual as expressed in the learning process.

Since, in didaction, the organizational elements that initiate action are intrinsic to the individual in a pre-didactic stage, it would seem to be impossible to schematize their expression. Expression of an original relationship with action is conceived in context on the basis of the knowledge of those who intervene and materials that can be used once action is initiated. The only thing certain is that inactivity is not didactive. The virtual screen is ready to depict action. No diagram, no model, no system can fully anticipate didaction. Personal projects to some extent determine a postsystemic action. Creation escapes the logic of systems and recasts them with each new relationship to a representation of the task.

Is creation not the locus of *différance*, of the possible reorganization of frames of reference, of the autonomous emergence of proprioceptive idiosyncracy? Can we tame creation in all its provocative nature, and didacticize it? Can we transpose it into a concatenation of discrete units? Or rather, can we *didactivate* it? What is this didaction, and what value does it have? How do we assess it? Can we, at last, *create* in education? But if so, how can we forecast creation? How can we organize intrinsic motivation? In the *trans-*didactics of language, literaction recognizes the cry from the heart as an act of intelligence.

Afterword:
The Myth of Security

This afterword is dedicated to the subject of education in low-tier schools and downhill trends in the educational system. First written before the events of September 11, 2001, it has since acquired a brand new perspective.[1] My starting point is John Devine's book *Maximum Security* (1996), which analyses competing discourses on violence within these high-security schools and boards of education. The intervenors whose experience Devine reports are tutors, mentors, and ethnographers, but a large role is played by school guards and scan teams in the construction of the 'indocile body' and students' relationship with their own bodies, to use Foucault's metaphors of the Panopticon and the gaze as foundational myths of security.

This is the first time I have encountered a description of New York schools 'at risk' that is at once detailed and linked to a reconceptualization of the processes that constitute these schools as a social problem. I have visited schools pretty well everywhere: in the French Caribbean, for instance, which, as a French *département*, achieves fourth place in national examinations; in Mexico, in classes that are both dynamic and disciplined; in the Andes, where children travel miles on foot to attend schools with dirt floors; in Africa and Asia, where children thirsting for culture revere the knowledge and the social roles that are handed on to them. But in urban, sometimes comfortable areas, problems can arise that have developed in a postmodern world. In Europe, students may roll their joints at the back of the class without eliciting a visible reaction from the teacher, and some institutions have toilets without doors, lights, and paper, as a result of damage caused by students. The urban context has prompted numerous attempts to preserve the integrity of the school, even to the point where complete isolation is viewed positively, as I witnessed in a South American Jewish high school which the principal had made into an oasis founded on moral values and project-based learning, by means of high walls and weapons detection at the entrance to protect the children.

Yet I have never encountered anything with the intensity of what is described in John Devine's *Maximum Security*. In the course of a narrative that is as fascinating as it is detailed, the author describes the universe of inner-city low-tier schools. His approach is of particular interest to me as I have been engaged in intervention/research on introspective tutoring in a disadvantaged setting. Nor am I unfamiliar with his environment: from time to time I visit the borders of Harlem near Columbia University, and seen dope dealers' contractors preparing crack in the streets. The ice-cream truck goes from street to street daily to collect the hits that have been prepared and to provide materials for the next day's supply. The whole time, its bell tinkles away, and it is followed from afar by a black Mercedes. The image of colonies of crack makers in the streets of Harlem may leave the impression of something close to a reconstituted social order that provides work to the destitute, a kind of social insurance for a country that has none. But witnessing the reality leaves me little inclined to ironic cynicism. Devine's description of the culture of violence that underlies this second-zone economy is so shocking it calls for reflection followed by action; for if this process perpetuates itself and spreads further, school culture may soon be replaced by a culture of terror, by virtue of the very measures taken to eradicate violence.

Maximum Security broaches a subject that has been foreclosed in American education. (In Lacanian psychology, foreclosure is the negation of a member of one's family whose existence one wants to forget.) Nobody seems to be interested in knowing the worst when the worst has become commonplace. Without being alarmist after his years of front-line experience, Devine conducts an in-depth analysis of the operation of schools whose record of academic failure puts them at the very bottom of the list. The jargon employed by boards of education is rife with euphemisms for the problem faced by these schools, and information on what really goes on there is often simply not conveyed. The reality of the situation will be disturbing as long as even the teachers who work in the schools see only one part of it, while the other part remains in the hands of the squads of school security guards. The fact is that, confronted with violence, the institution of the school has found no recourse other than technological escalation (e.g., walkie-talkies, weapons detectors). Devine shows the perverse effects of this response: the intrusion of the world of the penal into the 'school,' whose survival Devine puts into question through his use of quotation marks; the separation of the student's body and mind (one belongs to the guard, the other to the teacher); the fragmentation of the fields of intervention appropriate to the principal and teachers; the break between teaching and moral values; and the reversal of values for the student, since what is essential must take place in the school hallways.

John Devine conducts an ethnography of the hallways as well as of the classroom. In these hallways certain areas are reserved for the settling of scores, and are feared even by security guards. sometimes students have sex in the halls; sometimes they pee and defecate there because most of the toilets, which have become no more than sites of ambush, have been closed off. But the author is an intervenor before he is an ethnographer: he is a tutor and mentor before being a researcher. In this, he rejects 'detached' research of the kind that says, 'I've been there, this is how it is,' and positions himself as an agent in a universe of actors who are together constructing the meaning of what they experience. This co-construction occurs in the spaces where operate the team of tutors (students who have graduated) to 'at-risk students' (here, the dangers of stigmatization are flagged). It occurs in the seminar where they meet to debate, sometimes stormily, the violence they have been plunged into willy-nilly. And it occurs in the schools in the course of conversations with various participants in this universe.

Interviews objectify, and a countermethodology must be proposed: one of self-reflection rather than an incursion into the life of the other. This position consists of launching a dialogue between roles and processes, beliefs and epistemological universes, within an interracial ethic. In so doing, most of the traps currently denounced in social anthropology can be avoided. There aren't good schools on one side and bad schools on the other. Looking at two sectors of a single school, things can be both worse and better than they were five years ago. The social split seems to be created not so much by the adolescents them-selves as by the system that skims off the best, making life intolerable and education unmanageable in these low-tier schools.

These schools are the product of institutional decisions. The best educational initiatives, like that of creating smaller schools (Vision schools), are part of a system that organizes innovation to the detriment of the poorer schools, emptying these last of their best staff. Faced with this hopeless situation, which sees monies allotted to high-tech security systems instead of pedagogical training, the adolescent has no recourse but to adopt the belligerent mores of the street and bring them to school in order to learn – in the hallways – the basics of survival in the only world he or she still has access to. This learning process, labelled by newly arrived young immigrants as a process of Americanization, consists of learning to break the rules and to earn respect by being tougher than anyone else. It makes one wonder why this institutional system insists on teaching young people junior-high or late elementary-school math and English, instead of simply teaching them a trade, as is done for young people their age in other countries.

Despite the competence, devotion, and dedication of many teachers who devote nearly all their time to seeing that some of their students get a chance at success, responsibility for the social slippage inherent in the system can in part be laid at their door. This has been the object of debate within teachers' unions, and right- and left-wing political allegiances have not influenced the decisions made. Because of the frequency of legal action, the unions recommend that teachers no longer touch the students or intervene in their fights. It has become too dangerous; the insurance industry refuses to compensate injuries, and lawyers find it easy to turn the situation against teachers. In cases of conflict, it is recommended that the teacher not intervene but leave the classroom and call the security guard. Thus many teachers in these schools have abandoned a part of their role in moral instruction; they no longer impose discipline, and if they do try to indicate consequences, they become prey to threats and attacks.

This trend follows the general direction of fragmentation of the educational function already begun by the existence of para-educational specialties such as advisor, special educator, and so on. The technical distribution of responsibilities among different kinds of intervenor divides the intervention and prohibits a holistic settling of matters. The principal is deprived of control over his or her school, and the teacher loses the role of mentor, which, by virtue of the integration of the security guard into the local community, is now conferred on the latter through a curious role reversal: the guards know the students better, fraternize with them unofficially, and without overt acknowledgment gradually become the students' new models. Teachers, whose sphere of influence is restricted to the intellect, have quietly abandoned discipline and hardly play the role that was once associated with them any longer. In class, the kids are in control, and the rules change as soon as they are subject to a bit of pressure (which Devine calls the 'Marshmallow Effect').

What is the position of the teacher in the process of the sidelining of the body, values, and discipline? In Devine's reinterpretation of individual liberties and the mind-body relationship, violence is handled as the latest curricular specialty. His analysis of sexuality and a true-life case of abortion provide the springboard for an alternative view of youth culture, and for remythologizing inner-city schooling. John Devine weaves a demonstration. The effects of his moral position appear in the team work with tutors of varied races, nationalities, and beliefs. The epilogue gives voice to a fantasy which includes references to the stance of the postmodern avant-garde, about which the author reveals a clearheaded perceptiveness, revealing the possibility for exceeding it.

To say more would be to reveal the outcome of this narrative of experience, and possibly to instil a Derridean *différance* into a work that is very open and interracial. The author has a message to convey, resulting from the shattering experiment his team is conducting in extremely difficult neighbourhoods. Thanks to its practical rootedness in educational reality, and its final unveiling, this book is a posthumanist masterpiece.

Defining Teacherhood

The deconstruction in *Maximum Security* of currents specific to teacher education has thrown certain paradoxes into relief and led me to postulate the primacy of experience, providing experience respects a certain spirit. In line with chapters 3 and 4, in which I sought to explore solutions to problems previously raised – the confusion between words and action, ideology and change, economics and education – I would postulate that the vital wellspring of reflection is not argument, but reflection's fit with the acting mind. What is at issue is contact, not rationalization. Rather than articulating my definition on the basis of current research on teachers' professional competency – a focus of other publications – I have considered the question in a more philosophical light, by working from my examination of Indo-European mythos and in light of the Aristotelian perspective presented in chapter 4. I will base my demonstration on the premises laid out there, namely, that beams of meaning weave the fabric of the space of intelligence and characterize teacherhood. These beams determine cultural and social currents; they are the manifestation of the acting mind and play a constitutive role in teacherhood. Thus by definition, reflection can no longer be viewed as argument-based or taxonomic: rather, it is the mirror of the soul, the situating of a coming to awareness, a search for authenticity.

Recall that, within a certain neo-Aristotelian tradition of thought, meaning is defined as a space of action and intelligence, whether potential or actualized. The actualization of teacherhood in time is a manifestation of this mental space. Thus meaning is produced by the impact of intelligence on space and the reconstituted temporal linearity that results from it. In this perspective, the spaces of meaning are layered such that there is congruence among individuals who share an epistemic beam. Individuals close to each other geographically may yet not be in agreement, because they don't share the same conceptual beam. They are separated by signs and tied to specific symbolic systems. The forging of such a symbolic system, or of a linking metaphor, facilitates consensus and characterizes teacherhood. Teacherhood is born in the transmission of a beam of knowledge. Thanks to the acting mind, that active meaningfulness illuminates the passage to action from a state of potentiality. Teacherhood can therefore be viewed as an extension of the acting mind. The acting mind is not to be found in books; it is transmitted through contact, in action.

Let us try, then, to define the becoming of teacherhood. In the relation of subject to object, as well as in the relation of the subject to the self, one dimension appears to be lacking in this discussion that, if present, would explain the dynamic nature of the attraction that knowledge exerts. Teacherhood as becoming can be plausibly understood to draw its dynamism from love. Love sets up a principle of attraction that integrates both facets of being, that is, one's status as both object and subjective being. But let's translate love into language that is more academically acceptable (seemingly love has not yet had scientific legitimacy conferred upon it). There exists a conceptual current that integrates differences and elicits a variety of points of view, accommodating diversity in unity: it is humanism. I refer here not to the discourse of the God-fearing right (Apple, 2001), nor to its call for a return to the wellsprings of European tradition. Rather, I am referring to something that has freed itself from the cynical allure taken on by the sciences and the humanities in their role as the lackeys of financiers.

This something is a new, incarnate way of seeing, which is taking root in marked contrast to what has been seen as the academic mindset; its mindset is engaged rather than detached, creative rather than reactive. In the twenty-first century, with the predatory giants in the process of ripping the world apart, reaction against the bourgeois mind is no longer relevant. That struggle is over. The naive bourgeois middle class is in the process of being decimated, at least economically, along with the labouring classes that it never sought to help. In the face of overwhelming risks, when discussion among political leaders revolves around the legitimacy of using mini nuclear bombs to dislodge a billionaire buried at the heart of mazes of concrete, the only justifiable response is a paradigm shift. Human beings robbed of their power to act can take possession of the right to life by choosing to act in another way: to break free of canons and think differently without swearing fealty to Benetton or some high-tech company; to affirm the only value that is denied with vehemence by the academy – love, which expresses itself in humanism. Humanism is a way of thought that has given rise to an unparalleled variety of original and diverse concepts and that has stimulated the arts and the sciences by pointing towards their practical, eclectic purpose in developing humanity. And yet, it is not this humanism I want to talk about. Rather, it is the humanism of a Carl Rogers – if one must cite an authority – in the field not of psychology, but of teacherhood. Within a humanist paradigm, it appears justifiable to engage in science with a conscience and to advance that much despised value, love – despised because we have invoked it without living by it.

There's no need to present lengthy proofs of the misdeeds of conscienceless science. Our ecological problems have put humankind under a sword of Damocles; short-sighted economic approaches create one rich person for every twenty-nine who barely meet their expenses and seventy who are unequivocally poor. Currently, the economy is driven by social and international hostilities, neocolonialism being adroitly camouflaged by such terms as globalization. In contrast, ecologically minded thinking fits into a humanist paradigm. Economic thinking would also do so, if it followed the ecology-friendly approach proposed by Ivan Illich (1994). Humanism is the bearer of the values that are lacking in present-day science. Humanist reflection takes the long-term view. It allows opposed points of view to coexist and nourishes contradiction as a means of generating the greatest possible variety of expressions of human nature. Humanism does not consist of the dictatorship of conscience, but rather of a relativism that is democratic and concerned to respect diversity and difference.

So redefined, humanism constitutes the predisposition of conscience to free itself from paradoxes by resolving them in action and thought that give love its due place. What is in question is a summoning of the other and a call to mutualize experience. Love is the source of life. In humanism, the mind is perceived as immanent, springing forth from the human when human beings draw near to the truly human and recognize therein their own human identity. Evil then becomes the absence of communication, withdrawal into the self, a reason for excommunication from the group. Teacherhood is communication. The communicative act of Jürgen Habermas (1987) perhaps constituted a neo-Aristotelian revival. Intelligence is the act of communicating and is born from contact and reciprocity.

Groups of human beings are differentiated by beams of interest, and human beings take nourishment from the cultural beams that give them a social space. Teacherhood is the bearer of the meaning given to space; within it, contact with origins becomes a life narrative. Contact with the mind that enacts teacherhood partakes of the dynamics of energy, not of rational investigation. How does this contact, which characterizes teacherhood, play itself out? What is the link between the space of virtual meaning that seeks to manifest itself and the human being in search of contact? How does the acting mind manifest itself? How is teacherhood developed? One medium for this that stands out above all others is oral exchange, human contact. Oral exchange is used here in a holistic, semiotic sense: as word or speech, as symbolic transmission. The essential role of language in the transformation of acts was remarked upon in chapter 4, in reference to von Humboldt, and presented in action in chapter 5, in reference to action poetry. Meaning is actualized by the power of the word, which brings the sphere of the virtual contents of the universe into the perceptual space of their representation and dynamic implementation. That is where teacherhood is situated. Since representation consists of the passage to action and learning, it brings about the passage from education to character-building, which I call form-action (or active formation). In this perspective, symbols are the threshold manifestations of an act of speech. As von Humboldt suggested, language is action manifesting the creative initiative of the mind. Within every language, this action designates the locus of its manifestations. Thus the instrument of teacherhood is language, language whose expression elicits contact with the mind that underlies the symbols, through active formation. Teacherhood will maintain its power through awareness of the correspondence between an action and its mindset. Awareness of this correspondence will characterize contact and stimulate motivation. Intentionality, a teleological sense (a sense of goals), will thereby be reinforced. This is what I have referred to as 'didaction.'

Let's locate teacherhood in a postmodern space. Teacherhood occurs in situations. Situations are bearers of knowledge and have symbolic power. If, in a humanist perspective, evil is the absence of communication, teacherhood responds to social malaise. In that case, interlocal communication becomes politicized. The acting mind arrives at semiotic territoriality. Within the dynamics of cultural meaning, conceptual boundaries acquire political meaning. Cultural groups are brought together by theme-based mindsets. It is now more important than ever to recover teacherhood, to recover the sense of direction and the contact that is the vital role of the mind in communicative action. There exists a great risk that teacherhood will yield to the logic of the marketplace. Beams of meaning are hardening into turfs. Public meaning is becoming the property of lobby groups that usurp the powers of intercommunication and drive off thematic networks by systematically co-opting their key concepts for economic ends.

Teacherhood, that is, knowledge of the acting mind, constitutes a third space. It situates that dimension brought into evidence by Henri Lefebvre and contextualized by Edward Soja: a third space where everything comes together, subject and object, abstract and concrete, real and imaginary, knowable and unimaginable, daily life and unending history. Teacherhood is a manifestation of this other dimension, which in a sense is the heir to Kantian becoming. In educational situations, the acting mind explains the power of metaphors to model space by doubling back on the space of action. Perhaps these two movements are complementary, or perhaps there is no movement at all, movement being no more than a historicist illusion where nothing exists but space. Meaning vectors space by giving it a history. Semiotic, spatio-temporal consciousness[2] is not wholly circumscribed by material forms nor by isolated mental models. Their mutual actualization gives rise to the birth, through the substance of conceptual relationships, of meanings in the process of becoming, meanings that nourish energy and that are necessary to the maintenance of the acting mind. In teacherhood, meaning prevails over contingency, and life has a direction. In four-dimensional space-time, past, present, and future are all erased, giving access to the redimensionality envisaged by both Avicenna and Edward Soja. History is born of the order imposed on phenomena by the observer. It is possible to conceive that, in another dimensionality, the outlines of cohesion will be different. We no longer stand within an absolutely temporal perspective. Once time is made relative, it becomes regional: it depends on points of view that are geographic. For each observer, a relativized present traces the outlines of the elsewhere, the omega as the potentiality of the alpha, the initial intention that redefines teacherhood *a posteriori.*

In summary, then, these reflections have led me to specify the conditions for teacherhood. Teacherhood is born of knowledge of, and contact with, the acting mind, in line with a primary epistemic beam. Through access to this virtual space of intelligence, action becomes creation and communication. As action, teacherhood is the manifestation of intelligence in potentiality in an interactional situation, such that it gives vital meaning to that situation. It tends towards the political organization of space, with the purpose of transforming the spatio-temporal matrix that underpins meaning. Teacherhood is the bearer of becoming and conceives this becoming in the love of human beings. In teacherhood, communicative action is love. In this fact lie the foundations of all knowledge and of the possibility for progress.

The Ethical Dimension of Teacherhood

I could conclude by reflecting on the absence of such knowledge. Without it, it appears inevitable that protectionist measures be taken in the search for safety. That is because, at the highest levels, an entirely foreseeable situation related to the absence of communication between human beings has not really been understood nor taken into account. Thus the language of safety proves to be that of oppression, and individuals who choose safety at the expense of liberty, from fear and in good faith, do not realize that in so doing they curtail the possibility that has been opened up by the breach, the possibility of communicating with the other regarding what has gone wrong in their relations. This leads to the paradox that increased security measures rapidly become the main source of insecurity. Faced with mass phenomena like these, one can't help musing about the difficulties that human beings have in learning to be free and to respect others. That is precisely where teacherhood ought to situate itself.

In times of crisis, teachers are often closer to children than their own parents, serving as models and playing a stabilizing role socially. In experienced teachers, there is a subtle dynamic between logic and intuition (Atkinson & Claxton, 2000). As we saw, mediation occurs not just in relation to knowledge, but also in relation to experience. Experienced teachers share certain characteristics, such as the care they put into relations with their pupils, the quality and flexibility of their planning (because the human relationship has priority), the breadth of their knowledge and their motivation to broaden it further, and their skill at transforming pupils, by the very quality of the human relationships they develop. Empathy, the capacity to understand others, is not subject to measurement, but it is one of the factors that facilitate teaching. It marks the distinction between relationships based just on teaching-and-learning and relationships that emerge from 'transformative' teaching-and-learning (Robertson, 1996). Transformative teaching-and-learning is not just a stringing-together of knowledge; it transforms the paradigm with which the learner was reflecting at the outset. It consists of creative transformation, in the sense that Freire (1996) gives this term. Teachers can be perceived alternately as ideal models and non-people, enigmas and solutions, visionaries and interviewers, sources of frustration and of rewards. As a state of mind, teacherhood may be in the process of disappearing. Fewer and fewer people want to serve as models to others to help them build themselves up. The labour involved is just too hard; the problems are too grave. Sometimes teachers quit their jobs just by doing no more than what is essential. Some of them give children Ritalin to calm them down; their box of 'candies' is ever at hand on their desk. It's a simple matter of survival. Demand increases and it's almost impossible to respond. Social relations become so difficult that it is easier not even to manage certain kinds of problem. During times of crisis, the role filled by the teacher borders on the heroic: who could possibly take on such a level of commitment?

One remedy available to the teaching profession is to come together as a professional body, with a code of ethics and standards for social protection, as well as structures allowing for reflection in community-based small groups. Partnerships of this kind revive a sense of solidarity and make it possible to take a stand against the general derailment of values, by unveiling the processes of camouflage that give social aggression the appearance of justice and equity. In such a context, deconstruction takes on a dimension of positive resistance: it deciphers the discourse that underlies discourse, throws paradoxes into relief, and reveals the hidden stakes of financial forces that are imposing a direction on events while no one local interferes because the stakes are now global. Today, everything is for sale, and education is no exception (Magnusson, 2000). It is in the hope of buying comfort that citizens allow their representatives to spend billions of dollars; not in order to eradicate the hunger and injustice that prompt violence – something that could be accomplished with smaller sums – but in order to maintain their war machine and the pharmaceutical industry that screens it. Fear

and the spirit of revenge incite them to pass laws that are likely to
transform what had become a republic into a dictatorship, through a
quasi-democratic delegation of powers. What is left of citizenship when
citizens become minor pawns on an international chessboard? How shall
we win back the right to information and preserve the fundamental
rights of the citizen, no matter where she or he lives? How can we set up
a planet-wide democracy?

Massarenti's (1989) theory of paired parameters is worth revisiting in
light of current events. Massarenti advances an analysis of the concepts
of strength and fear, psychological violence, and legitimized (state)
violence, by examining the parameters of changing attitudes. Unimaginable actions emerge when human misery is such that there is nothing
left to lose. As he puts it, to eliminate kamikaze action, everyone must be
granted the following, provided for under the Universal Declaration of
Human Rights:

– Social security (under Article 22): The right of all to economic,
  social, and cultural support, through the efforts of all, in all places.
– Work (under Article 23): Free choice of employment, good conditions of work, protection against unemployment, and equal and just
  pay for equal work.
– Standard of living (under Article 25): The right to a standard of
  living adequate for the health and well-being of oneself and one's
  family, including food, clothing, housing, and medical care, as well
  as support in the event of widowhood and in old age.
– Social order (under Article 28): The right to a social order around
  the world that enables recognition and respect for rights and
  freedoms.
– Duties (under Article 29): Everyone has the duty to ensure the
  freedom, equality, and peace of others in the society he or she lives
  in. (Massarenti, 1989, trans. Rina Kampeas). To this end, 'selfishness
  must be combated and governments must voluntarily divert half
  of the hundreds of millions they now spend on armaments towards
  the attainment of this goal,' peace among peoples (L. Massarenti,
  personal communication, 2002).

You would think principles like these would be elementary and that
everyone would agree on their significance, yet we have not yet implemented the conditions for their fulfilment. Will humanity be obliged to
attain a better balance between rich and poor only at the price of the

collapse of an economic system whose hypocritical double standards have become flagrant? Whatever the case, teachers are playing a greater role than ever in raising awareness. Their role is moral, grounded in service to others (van Manen, 2000). To close I can only quote the words of Jacques Delors to the Council of Europe (1996, pp. 157–8): 'The importance of the role of the teacher as an agent for change who promotes mutual understanding and tolerance has never been as clear as it is today. This role will no doubt be still more decisive in the twenty-first century. Narrow nationalisms will have to give place to universalism and ethnic and cultural prejudices to tolerance, understanding, and pluralism; and totalitarianism will have to be replaced by democracy ... This imperative imposes enormous responsibility on teachers, who work together to form the characters and minds of the next generation. The stakes are high and they make the moral values acquired during child-hood and throughout life our top priority.'

Notes

Introduction

1 See <http://www.atwoodpublishing.com> for the *International Journal of Applied Semiotics,* and <http://labweb.education.wisc.edu/semiotics/> for the special interest group in semiotics and education.

Chapter 1: Myths in Teacher Education

1 An early version of this chapter was published in the journal *Pedagogy, Culture and Society,* 7(2), 1999, with the title 'Myths in teacher education: Towards reflexivity.'

2 I dare say education covers all three of these fundamental aspects of life. This Indo-European tripartition emerges in work that applies the methods of comparative grammar to mythology (Dumézil, 1941). It would seem to have been preceded by an earlier stage in which were found four castes or *varnas.*

3 In this respect, the purpose of mastery learning does not seem so different from those of other major families of instructional models, such as more inductive approaches to instruction. In connection with the inductive/deductive debate, it should be remembered that research on sequencing organizers and instructional synthesizers indicates that, with the tools currently used in research, it is not possible to make a replicable, scientific comparison of deductive and inductive sequencing in various classroom settings (Tochon, 1990a). Moreover, the properties of induction and of deduction respectively are subject to debate.

4 The same argument could be made in the other direction: practitioners use simple words to reflect practical arguments (Fenstermacher, 1994), and researchers have a hard time second-guessing what field realities are represented by the practitioners.

Chapter 2: Deconstructing Presence

1 An early version of this chapter was published in the journal *Curriculum Studies* (Tochon, 1994).

Chapter 3: The Situated Researcher and the Myth of Lived Experience

1 An early version of this chapter was published in *International Journal of Applied Semiotics* (Tochon, 1996b).
2 Not to speak of this note, written in the United States.

Chapter 4: Exploring Educational Spaces

1 An earlier version of this text was presented at the symposium 'Thirdspace: The Semiotics of Space, Place, Substance, and Relationships' during the annual meeting of the Semiotic Society of America (SSA), Toronto, Ontario, October 15–18, 1998, and gathered in the acts of the symposium, Semiotics and third space, edited by Linda Rogers (Madison, WI: Atwood Publishing, 2002).
2 It should be recalled that Aristotle, the son of the physician to the king of Macedonia, was first Plato's disciple, then his rival, and preserved a marked admiration and respect for him.

Chapter 5: A Manifesto for Didaction

1 I presented the debate around this issue and the experiences from French-speaking Switzerland and Northern Ontario in the journal *Arts and Learning Research* (Tochon, 2000a).
2 The English reader should note that the sounds of *si on* ('if we') are the same as those of *scions* ('let us saw') with the implicit metaphor of the jail bars alluding to freedom of speech, and to speaking in French while English is the language of the majority and the well-off.

Afterword

1 Aspects of this chapter have been published in *Curriculum Studies* (Tochon, 1998) and in *Carrefours de l'éducation* (Tochon, 2001b).
2 'Semiotic consciousness' was the title given to a special issue of the *International Journal of Applied Semiotics* (Tochon, 2002b).

References

Aguirre, A., Jr. (2000). *Women and minority faculty in the academic workplace: Recruitment, retention, and academic culture.* Washington, DC: ERIC Clearinghouse on Higher Education. (ERIC Digest No. ED446723)

Amoa, B. (1994). L'atelier de poésie du griot [The griot's poetry workshop]. *Revue de Linguistique appliquée, 93,* 62–77.

Anderson, J.R. (1983). *The architecture of cognition.* Cambridge, MA: Harvard University Press.

Anderson, L.W. (1996, April). *A quarter-century of mastery learning: Lessons learned from Johnson City, New York.* Paper presented at the annual meeting of the American Educational Reseach Association (AERA), New York.

Apple, M.W. (2000). The shock of the real: Critical pedagogies and rightist reconstructions. In P.P. Trifonas (Ed.), *Revolutionary pedagogies: Cultural politics, instituting education, and the discourse of theory* (pp. 225–50). New York: RoutledgeFalmer.

Apple, M.W. (2001). *Educating the 'right' way: Markets, standards, God, and inequality.* New York: RoutledgeFalmer.

Atkinson, T., & Claxton, G. (2000). *The intuitive practitioner: On the value of not always knowing what one is doing.* London: Open University Press.

Bachelard, G. (1932). *L'intuition de l'instant* [The instant intuition]. Paris: Gonthier.

Bakhtin, M. (1981). *The dialogical imagination: Four essays by M.M. Bakhtin* (M. Holquist, Ed.). Austin: University of Texas Press.

Barone, T. (1992a, April). *The limits of theory: Critical storytelling and the deep persuasion of the polity.* Paper presented at the annual meeting of the American Educational Reseach Association (AERA), San Francisco.

Barone, T. (1992b, April). *Persuasive authors, skeptical readers, powerless characters: Goodness in story telling.* Paper presented at the annual meeting of the American Educational Research Association (AERA), San Francisco.

Barone, T. (2001). *Touching eternity: The enduring outcomes of teaching.* New York: Teachers College Press.

Barthes, R. (1967). *Système de la mode* [The fashion system]. Paris: Seuil.

Barthes, R. (1973). *Le plaisir du texte* [The pleasure of the text]. Paris: Seuil.

Bereiter, C. (1991). Implications of connectionism for thinking about rules. *Educational Researcher, 20*(3), 10–16.

Bernstein, R.J. (1983). *Beyond objectivism and relativism: Science, hermeneutics and praxis.* Philadelphia: University of Pennsylvania Press.

Bertrand, Y., & Houssaye, J. (1999). Pédagogie and didactique: An incestuous relationship. *Instructional Science: An international journal of learning and cognition, 27*(1–2), 33–51.

Bibby, P.A. (1992). Distributed knowledge – In the head, in the world. In Y. Rogers, A. Rutherford, & P.A. Bibby (Eds.), *Models in the mind: Theory, perspective and application* (pp. 93–100). New York: Academic Press.

Blanchard-Laville, C., & Fablet, D. (1998). *Analyser les pratiques professionnelles* [Analysing professional practices]. Paris: L'Harmattan.

Block, J., & Burns, R. (1976). Mastery learning. In L.S. Shulman (Ed.), *Review of research in education* (Vol. 4, pp. 3–31). Itasca, IL: Peacock.

Bloom, B.S. (1984). The 2–sigma problem: The search for methods of group instruction as effective as one-to-one tutoring. *Educational Researcher, 13,* 4–16.

Bloom, B.S., Hastings, J.T., & Madaus, G.F. (1971). *Handbook on formative and summative evaluation of student learning.* New York: McGraw-Hill.

Bruner, J. (1986). *Actual minds, possible worlds.* Cambridge, MA: Harvard University Press.

Bruner, J. (1990). *Acts of meaning.* Cambridge: Harvard University Press.

Buchmann, M. (1992, April). *Figuring in the past: Thinking about teacher memories.* Paper presented at the annual meeting of the American Educational Research Association (AERA), San Francisco.

Buckley, P.K., & Cooper, J.M. (1978, March). *An ethnographic account study of an elementary schoolteacher's establishment and maintenance of group norms.* Paper presented at the annual meeting of the American Educational Research Association (AERA), Toronto.

Burns, R. (1992, April). *Why the future of mastery learning research points to the past.* Paper presented at the annual meeting of the American Educational Reseach Association (AERA), San Francisco.

Carroll, J. (1963). A model of school learning. *Teachers College Record, 64,* 723–33.

Carroll, J. (1989). The Carroll model: A 25–year retrospective and prospective view. *Educational Researcher, 18,* 26–31.

Castells, M. (1977). *The urban question.* London: Arnold.

Chandler, S. (1992). Displaying our lives: An argument against displaying our theories. *Theory into Practice, 31*(2), 126–31.

Chevallard, Y. (1999). Didactique? Is it a plaisanterie? You must be joking! A critical comment on vocabulary. *Instructional Science,* 27(1), 2–3.

Chliwniak, L. (1997). *Higher education leadership: Analyzing the gender gap.* Washington, DC: George Washington University. (ERIC Digest No. ED410846)

Clancey, W.J. (1992, April). *'Situated' means coordinating without deliberation.* Paper presented at the annual meeting of the American Educational Reseach Association (AERA), San Francisco.

Clandinin, D.J. (1991, April). *Teacher education as narrative inquiry.* Paper presented at the annual meeting of the American Educational Research Association (AERA), Chicago.

Clandinin, D.J., & Connelly, E.M. (1989a). *Narrative and story in practice and research.* Toronto: Ontario Institute for Studies in Education. Research report.

Clandinin, D.J., & Connelly, E.M. (1989b). *Personal knowledge in curriculum.* Toronto: Ontario Institute for Studies in Education. Research report.

Clandinin, D.J., & Connelly, E.M. (1996). Teachers' professional knowledge landscapes: Teacher stories – Stories of teachers – School stories – stories of schools. *Educational Researcher, 25*(3), 24.

Cochran-Smith, M., & Fries, M.K. (2001). Sticks, stones, and ideology: the discourse of reform in teacher education. *Educational Researcher, 30*(8), 3–15.

Cochran-Smith, M., & Lytle, S.L. (1999). The teacher research movement: A decade later. *Educational Researcher, 28*(7), 15–25.

Connelly, E.M., & Clandinin, D.J. (1988). *Teachers as curriculum planners: Narratives of experience.* Toronto: Ontario Institute for Studies in Education Press (co-published at Teacher's College Press, NY)

Connelly, E.M., & Clandinin, D.J. (1990). Stories of experience and narrative inquiry. *Educational Researcher, 19*(4), 2–14.

Connelly, E.M., & Clandinin, D.J. (1995). Narrative and education. *Teachers and Teaching: Theory and Practice, 1*(1), 73–86.

Coquet, J.C. (1985). Éléments de bio-bibliographie [Bibliographic elements]. In H. Parret & H.G. Ruprecht (Eds), *Essays in honor of A.J. Greimas* (pp. liii–lxxxv). Amsterdam: Benjamins.

Csikszentmihalyi, M., & Csikszentmihalyi, I.S. (1988). *Optimal experience: Psychological studies of flow in consciousness.* Cambridge: Cambridge University Press.

Dalpé, J.M. (1983). *Les murs de nos villages* [The walls of our villages]. Sudbury, ON: Prise de Parole.

Dalpé, J.M. (1984a). *Ceux d'ici* [Those who come from here]. Sudbury, ON: Prise de Parole.

Dalpé, J.M. (1984b). *Et d'ailleurs* [And from elsewhere]. Sudbury, ON: Prise de Parole.

Danesi, M. (1999a). *Encyclopedic dictionary of semiotics, media and communications.* Toronto: University of Toronto Press.

Danesi, M. (1999b). *Of cigarettes, high heels, and other interesting things: An introduction to semiotics.* New York: St Martin's Press.

Delors, J. (1996). *L'éducation. Un trésor est caché dedans* [Education: A treasure hides within]. Report to UNESCO of the International Commission on Education for the Twenty-first Century. Paris: UNESCO.

Derrida, J. (1976). *Of grammatology* (G.C. Spivak, Trans.). Baltimore: Johns Hopkins University Press. (Original work published 1967)

Derrida, J. (1978). *Writing and difference.* Chicago: University of Chicago Press.

Devine, J. (1996). *Maximum Security: The culture of violence in inner-city schools.* Chicago: University of Chicago Press.

Di Pardo, A. (1990). Narrative knowers, expository knowledge: Discourse as a dialectic. *Written Communication, 7,* 59–95.

Dumas, J. (1990, August). *Analyse d'un poème de Dalpé* [Analysis of a poem by Dalpé]. Sudbury, ON: Ontario Institute for Studies in Education, Centre de recherches en éducation du Nouvel-Ontario. Report.

Dumézil, G. (1941). *Jupiter, Mars, Quirinus.* Paris: Champion.

Eco, U. (1992). *Les limites de l'interprétation* [The limits of interpretation]. Paris: Grasset.

Eco, U., Santambrogio, M., & Violi, P. (1988). *Meaning and mental representations.* Bloomington: Indiana University Press.

Eisner, E. (1991). *The enlightened eye: On doing qualitative inquiry.* New York: Macmillan.

Elbaz, E. (1991). Research on teachers' knowledge: The evolution of a discourse. *Journal of Curriculum Studies, 23*(1), 1–19.

Ericsson, K.A., & Simon, H.A. (1994). *Protocol analysis: Verbal reports as data* (2nd ed.). Cambridge, MA: MIT Press.

Fenstermacher, G. (1994). The place of practical argument in the education of teachers. In V. Richardson (Ed.), *Teacher change and the staff development process* (pp. 23–42). New York: Teachers College Press, Teachers College, Columbia University.

Feyerabend, P. (1975). *Against method.* London: New Left Books.

Fitte-Duval, G.G. (1992). Intervention des griots de la Martinique [How griots from Martinique intervene]. *Les Ateliers du Sud-Est, 28,* 30–2.

Flaubert, G. (1876). *Les trois contes* [Three stories]. Paris: Garnier-Flammarion.

Foucault, M. (1980). *Power/knowledge: Selected interviews and other writing, 1972–1977.* New York: Pantheon.

Foucault, M. (1986). Of other spaces. *Diacritics, 16*, 22–7.

Freire, P. (1996). *Letters to Christina: Reflections on my life and work.* New York: Routledge.

Fugère, J. (1989). Jean-Marc Dalpé – L'urgence de se dire [Jean-Marc Dalpé: Self-talk as emergency]. *Liaison, 53*, 28–30.

Galisson, R. (1985). Didactologies et idéologies [Didactologies and ideologies]. *Études de Linguistique appliquée, 60*, 5–16.

Gambone, M.A. & Connell, J.P. (1998). *Theories of change approach to evaluate urban school-site reforming to scale.* Paper presented at the annual meeting of the American Educational Research Association (AERA), San Diego, CA.

Gardner, H. (1993). Halting the spread of educational fraud and deception. *Chronicle of Higher Education, 39*(19), B3.

Garfinkel, H. (1967). *Studies in ethnomethodology.* Englewood, Cliffs, NJ: Prentice-Hall.

Garner, R. (1987). *Metacognition and reading comprehension.* Norwood, NJ: Ablex.

Genette, G. (1983). *Nouveau discours du récit* [New discourse on the narrative]. Paris: Seuil.

Giddens, A. (1981). *A contemporary critique of historical materialism.* Berkeley: University of California Press.

Gomez, M.L., & Tabachnick, B.R. (1992, April). *Telling teaching stories.* Paper presented at the annual meeting of the American Educational Research Association (AERA), San Francisco.

Greimas, A.J. (1983). *Structural semantics.* Lincoln: University of Nebraska Press.

Greimas, A.J., & Courtés, J. (1989). The cognitive dimension of narrative discourse. *New Literary History, 20*(3), 563–79.

Gundem, B.B. (1992, April). *The place of didactics in curriculum in Scandinavia.* Paper presented at the annual meeting of the American Educational Research Association (AERA). San Francisco.

Guskey, T.R., & Gates, S.L. (1985, April). *A synthesis of research on group-based mastery learning programs.* Paper presented at the annual meeting of the American Educational Reseach Association (AERA), Chicago. (ERIC No. ED262088)

Guskey, T.R. (1994, April). *Clarifying outcome-based education and mastery learning.* Paper presented at the annual meeting of the American Educational Reseach Association (AERA), New Orleans, LA.

Habermas, J. (1987). *The theory of communicative action: Vol. 2. The critique of functionalist reason* (T. McCarthy, Trans.). Boston: Beacon Press. (Original work published 1981)

Habermas, J. (1990). Remarks on the discussion. *Theory, Culture and Society, 7*(4) 127–32.

Hall, E.T. (1959). *The silent language.* Garden City, NJ: Doubleday.

Hall, E. (1983). *The dance of life.* New York: Anchor/Doubleday.

Hargreaves, A. (1989). *Teachers' work and the politics of time and space.* Toronto: Ontario Institute for Studies in Education. Research report.

Harland, R. (1987). *Superstructuralism: The philosophy of structuralism and post-structuralism.* New York: Methuen.

Hlynka, D. (1989). Making waves with educational technology: A deconstructionist reading of Ted Aoki. *Journal of Curriculum Theorizing, 9*(2), 27–38.

Holland, J.H., Holyoak, K.J., Nisbett, R.E., & Thagard, P.R. (1986). *Induction: Processes of inference, learning, and discovery.* Cambridge, MA: MIT Press.

Hopmann, S. (1992, April). *Starting a dialogue: Roots and issues of the beginning conversation between European Didaktik and the American curriculum tradition.* Paper presented at the annual meeting of the American Educational Research Association (AERA), San Francisco.

Houssaye, J. (1994, April). *The relevance of the pedagogical triangle: Understanding operating principles of the pedagogical situation.* Paper presented at the annual meeting of the American Educational Research Association (AERA). New Orleans, LA.

Illich, I. (1994). *Dans le miroir du passé: Conférences et discours, 1978–1990* [In the mirror of the past: Lectures and presentations, 1978–1990] Paris: Descartes, trans. Maud Sissung and Marc Duchamp. Original publication 1992.

Jackson, P.W. (1968). *Life in classrooms.* New York: Holt, Rinehart & Winston.

Jahn, R.G., & Dunne, B.J. (1987). *Margins of reality: The role of consciousness in the physical world.* Orlando, FL: Harvest/Harcourt, Brace, Jovanovich.

Johnson-Laird, P.N., & Byrne, R.M.J. (1991). *Deduction.* Hillsdale, NJ: Erlbaum.

Jones, B.F., & Idol, I. (1990). *The dimensions of thinking and cognitive instruction.* Hillsdale, NJ: Erlbaum.

Jones, B.F., Palincsar, A.S., Ogle, D.S., & Carr, E.G. (1987). *Strategic teaching: Cognitive instruction in the content areas.* Alexandria, VA: Association for Supervision and Curriculum Development.

Joy, M. (1997). *Paul Ricoeur and narrative: Context and contestation.* Calgary, AB: University of Calgary Press.

Jung, C.G. (1964). *Dialectique du moi et de l'inconscient* [Dialectic of the ego and the unconscious]. Paris: Gallimard.

Kaestle, C.F. (1993). The awful reputation of education research. *Educational Researcher, 22*(1), 23–31.

Krathwohl, D., Bloom, B.S., & Masia, B.B. (1964). *Taxonomy of educational objectives: The classification of educational goals: Handbook 2. Affective domain.* New York: David McKay.

Kristeva, J. (2001). *Hannah Arendt: Life is a narrative.* Toronto: University of Toronto Press.

Kuhn, T.S. (1962). *The structure of scientific revolutions.* Chicago: University of Chicago Press.

Kulik, C.L., Kulik, J.A., & Bangert-Drowns, R.L. (1990). Effectiveness of mastery learning programs: A meta-analysis. *Review of Educational Research, 60*(2), 265–99.

Labov, W., & Waletsky, R. (1967). Narrative analysis: Oral versions of personal experience. In American Ethnological Society (J. Helm, Ed.), *Essays on the verbal and visual arts.* Seattle: University of Washington Press.

Lacotte, J., & Lenoir, Y. (1999). Didactics and professional practice in preservice teacher education: A comparison of the situation in two French-speaking states (France and Quebec). *Instructional Science, 27*(1), 181–239.

Ladson-Billings, G. (2001). *Crossing over to Canaan: The journey of new teachers in diverse classrooms.* San Francisco: Jossey-Bass.

Lather, P. (1989). Ideology and methodological attitude. *Journal of Curriculum Theorizing, 9*(2), 7–26.

Lather, P. (1992). Critical frames in educational research: Feminist and post-structural perspectives. *Theory into Practice, 31*(2), 1–13.

Lather, P., & Smithies, C. (1997). Troubling the angels: Women living with HIV/AIDS. Boulder, CO: Westview Press.

Latour, B. (1996). Sur la pratique des théoriciens [On theoreticians' practice]. In J.-M. Barbier (Ed.), *Savoirs théoriques et savoirs d'action* [Theoretical knowledge and knowledge from action] (pp. 131–46). Paris: Presses Universitaires de France.

Lefebvre, H. (1991). *The production of space* (D. Nicholson-Smith, Trans.). Cambridge: Blackwell.

Lévy, P. (1997). *L'intelligence collective: Pour une anthropologie du cyberspace* [Collective inteligence: For an anthropology of cyberspace]. Paris: La Découverte.

Lord, A.B. (1965). *The singer of tales.* Cambridge, MA: Harvard University Press.

Lyotard, J.-F. (1993). Excerpts from 'The postmodern condition: A report on knowledge.' In J. Natoli & L. Hutcheon (Eds.), *A postmodern reader* (pp. 71–90). Albany: State University of New York Press.

MacLure, M., & Stronach, I. (1992, April). *Jack in two boxes: A postmodern perspective on the transformation of persons into portraits.* Paper presented at the annual meeting of the American Educational Reseach Association (AERA), San Francisco.

Maddox, D. (1989). Veridiction, verifiction, verifactions: Reflections on methodology. *New Literary History, 20*(3), 661–78.

Magnusson, J.L. (1999). Five easy games of referencing. *International Journal of Applied Semiotics, 1*, (special issue), 45–56.

Magnusson, J.L. (2000). Examining higher education and citizenship in a global context of neoliberal restructuring. *Canadian Ethnic Studies, 32*(1), 1–17.

Martin, M.C. (1985a, March 6). Et voici les affiches-poèmes! [Here are the poster-poems!]. *La Suisse* (Geneva), [The 'Internationale' of Love – Poem in hand (or Poem punches?)]

Martin, M.C. (1985b, December 22). Internationale de l'amour – Poème au poing [The 'Internationale' of love: Poem punches]. *La Suisse* Geneva.

Marzano, R.J. (1991). Language, the language arts, and thinking. In J. Flood, J.M. Jensen, D. Lapp, & J.M. Squire (Eds.), *Handbook of research on teaching the English language arts* (pp. 559–86). New York: Macmillan.

Marzano, R.J., Brandt, R.S., Hugues, C.S., Jones, B.F., Presseisen, B.Z., Rankin, S.C., et al. (1988). *Dimensions of thinking: A framework for curriculum and instruction*. Alexandria, VA: Association for Supervision and Curriculum Development.

Massarenti, L. (1989). Une pédagogie des droits de l'homme: Un levain pour la paix [A pedagogy of human rights: A seed of peace]. *Cahiers de la Section des Sciences de l'Éducation, 57*. Geneva: Université de Genève, Faculté de Psychologie et des Sciences de l'Éducation.

Matter, H.L. (1985, March). Poésie – Un coup de Tochon. *L'Illustré, 12*, 64.

McClelland, J.L., & Rumelhart, D.E. (1988). *Explorations in parallel distributed processing: A handbook of models, programs, and exercises*. Cambridge, MA: MIT Press.

McDermott, R.P. (1976). *Kids make sense: An ethnographic account of the interactional management of success and failure in one first-grade classroom*. Unpublished doctoral dissertation. Stanford University, Stanford, CA.

McKeachie, W.J., Pintrich, P., Lin, Y.-G., & Smith, D. (1988). *Teaching and learning in the college classroom: A review of the research literature*. Ann Arbor: University of Michigan, National Center for Research to Improve Postsecondary Teaching and Learning. Report.

McLaren, P. (1998). Semioticizing the self: Social and cultural therapy as transformation. In L. Rogers (Ed.), *Wish I were: Felt pathways of the self* (pp. xiii–xvi). Madison, WI: Atwood.

Meier, D. (2000). *Will standards save public education?* Boston: Beacon Press.

Merleau-Ponty, M. (1962). *Phenomenology of perception* (Colin Smith, Trans.). New York: Routledge.

Monk, G., Winslade, J., Crocket, K., & Epston, D. (1997). *Narrative therapy in practice: The archaeology of hope*. San Francisco: Jossey-Bass.

Morin, E. (1967). *Pour une politique de l'Homme* [For a politics of the human]. Paris: Seuil.

Newell, A., & Simon, H.A. (1972). *Human problem-solving.* Englewood Cliffs, NJ: Prentice-Hall.

Ouellette, L.-M. (1996). *La communication au coeur de l'évaluation en formation continue* [Communication at the heart of evaluation in professional development]. Paris: Presses Universitaires de France.

Paden, J.N., & Soja, E.W. (1970). *The African experience: Vol. 2. Syllabus.* Evanston, IL: Northwestern University Press.

Perrenoud, P. (1988). Nouvelles didactiques et stratégies des élèves face au travail scolaire [New didactics and students' strategies in schoolwork]. In P. Perrenoud & C. Montandon (Eds.), *Qui maîtrise l'école? Politiques d'institutions et pratiques des acteurs* [Who masters school? Institutional policies and practices of agents] (pp. 175–95). Lausanne: Réalités sociales.

Perron, P., & Danesi, M. (1993). *A.J. Greimas and narrative cognition.* Toronto: University of Toronto, Victoria College, Toronto Semiotic Circle.

Piaget, J. (1974). *La prise de conscience* [Consciousness raising]. Paris: Presses Universitaires de France.

Pinar, W.F., & Bower, C.A. (1992). Politics of curriculum: Origins, controversies, and significance of critical perspectives. *Review of Research in Education, 18*(1), 163–90.

Pinar, W.F., Reynolds, W.M., Slattery, P., & Taubman, P.M. (1995). *Understanding curriculum: An introduction to the study of hisorical and contemporary curriculum discourses.* New York: Peter Lang.

Polanyi, M. (1962). *Personal knowledge: Towards a post-critical philosophy.* Chicago: University of Chicago Press.

Popkewitz, T.S. (1998). *Struggling for the soul: The politics of schooling and the construction of the teacher.* New York: Teachers College Press.

Popper, K. (1974). *Unended quest: An intellectual autobiography.* Glasgow, U.K.: Collins.

Poulantzas, N. (1978). *State, power, socialism.* London: Verso.

Primozic, D.T. (2001). *On Merleau-Ponty.* Belmont, CA: Wadsworth.

Propp, V. (1928). *Morfologija skazki* [Morphology of tales]. Leningrad: Akademia.

Proust, M. (1993). *A la recherche du temps perdu* [Remembrance of things past]. Paris: Hachette.

Resnick, L.B., & Klopfer, L.E. (1989). Toward the thinking curriculum: An overview. In L.B. Resnick & L.E. Klopfer (Ed.), *Toward the thinking curriculum: Current cognitive research* (pp. 1–19). Alexandria, VA: Association for Supervision and Curriculum Development.

Ricoeur, P. (1984–8). *Time and narrative* (Vols. 1–3). Chicago: University of Chicago Press.

Ricoeur, P. (1990). *Soi-même comme un autre* [Self as Another]. Paris: Seuil.

Robertson, D.L. (1996). Facilitating transformative learning: Attending to the dynamics of the educational helping relationship. *Adult Education Quarterly, 47*(1), 41–53.

Rogers, L. (1998). *Wish I were: Felt pathways of the self.* Madison, WI: Atwood.

Roth, D. (1983). Prix littéraires [Literary prizes]. *Le Nouvel Humaniste, 3,* 3.

Russell, R., Mawhinney, H., Banks, C., & Ortiz, F. (1998, April). *Are we working without a net? Can the care voice be heard in an era of restructuring?* Paper presented at the annual meeting of the American Educational Reseach Association (AERA), San Diego, CA.

Sacks, P. (1999). *Standardized minds: The high price of America's testing culture and what we can do to change it.* Cambridge, MA: Perseus Books.

Sapir, E. (1968). *Linguistics.* Paris: Minuit.

Sapir, E. (1989). *Collected works of Edward Sapir: Vol. 1. General linguistics* (P. Sapir, Chief Ed.; W. Bright, R. Darnell, V. Golla, E. Hamp, R. Handler, and J.T. Irvine, Eds.). Berlin: Mouton.

Scholes, R. (1985). *Textual power.* New Haven, CT: Yale University Press.

Schutz, A. (1967). *The phenomenology of the social world.* Evanston, IL: Northwestern University Press.

Schutz, A. (1987). *Le chercheur et le quotidien* [Researching daily activities]. Paris: Klincksieck.

Sebeok, T.A. (1991). *A sign is just a sign.* Bloomington: Indiana University Press.

Segal, J.W., Chipman, S.F., & Glaser, R. (1985). *Thinking and learning skills: Vol. 2. Relating instruction to research.* Hillsdale, NJ: Erlbaum.

Seidman, I. (1991). *Interviewing as qualitative research.* New York: Teachers College Press.

Slavin, R.E. (1987). Mastery learning reconsidered. *Review of Educational Research, 57,* 175–213.

Slavin, R.E. (1990). Mastery learning re-reconsidered. *Review of Educational Research, 60*(2), 300–2.

Smyth, J. (1992). Teachers' work and the politics of reflection. *American Educational Research Journal, 29*(2), 267–300.

Soja, E.W. (1968). *The geography of modernization in Kenya: A spatial analysis of social, economic, and political change.* Syracuse geographical series: No. 2. Syracuse, NY: Syracuse University Press.

Soja, E.W. (1971). *The political organization of space* (Resource Paper No. 8). Washington, DC: Association of American Geographers, Commission of College Geography.

Soja, E.W. (1989). *Postmodern geographies: The reassertion of space in critical social theory.* New York: Verso.

Soja, E.W. (1996). *Thirdspace: Journeys to Los Angeles and other real-and-imagined places.* Padstow, U.K.: Blackwell.

Sola, E. (1987). François Victor Tochon, un homme des arts [François Victor Tochon, a learned artist]. *Educateur, 1,* 27.

Solway, D. (1999). Outcomes based education: A referential tragedy. *International Journal of Applied Semiotics, 1*(special issue), 61–70.

Spivak, G.C. (1976). Introduction. In J. Derrida, *Of grammatology.* Baltimore: Johns Hopkins University Press.

Symonds, W.C. (2001, March 19). How to fix America's schools. *Business Week.*

Tassé, R. (1990). Jean-Marc Dalpé, poète – Voir le dessous des dessus [Jean-Marc Dalpé, poet: See the underside of the above]. *Le Temps, 5,* 2–3.

Tochon, F.V. (1985a, November). *Un poème pour la vie* [Life lines]. Unpublished manuscript.

Tochon, F.V. (1985b). *77 poèmes d'amour* [77 love poems]. Paris: Helios.

Tochon, F.-V. (1990a) Les cartes de concepts dans la recherche cognitive sur l'apprentissage et l'enseignement [Concept maps in cognitive research on learning and teaching]. *Perspectives documentaires en sciences de l'éducation, 21,* 87–106.

Tochon, F.-V. (1990b). *Didactique du français – De la planification à ses organisateurs cognitifs* [French didactics: From its planning to its cognitive organizers]. Paris: Éditions Sociales Françaises.

Tochon, F.V. (1990c). Heuristic schemata as tools for the epistemic analysis of teachers' thinking. *Teaching and Teacher Education, 6*(2), 183–96.

Tochon, F.V. (1991). *L'enseignement stratégique – Transformation pragmatique de la connaissance dans la pensée des enseignants* [Strategic teaching: A pragmatic transformation of knowledge in teachers' thinking]. Toulouse: Editions Universitaires du Sud.

Tochon, F.-V. (1994). Presence beyond the narrative: Semiotic tools for deconstructing the personal story. *Curriculum Studies, 2*(2), 221–45.

Tochon, F.V. (1998). Review of John Devine, *Maximum security. Journal of Curriculum Studies, 30*(4), 479–82.

Tochon, F.V. (1999a). Semiotic foundations for building the New Didactics: An introduction to the prototype features of the discipline. *Instructional Science: An International Journal of Learning and Cognition, 27*(1–2), 9–32.

Tochon, F.V. (1999b). The situated researcher and the narrative reference to lived experience. *International Journal of Applied Semiotics, 1*(special issue), 103–14.

Tochon, F.V. (1999c). *Video Study Groups for Education, Development, and Change.* Madison, WI: Atwood.

Tochon, F.V. (2000a). Action poetry as an empowering art: A manifesto for didaction in arts education. *Arts and Learning Research Journal, 16*(1), 32–53.

Tochon, F.V. (2000b). When authentic experiences are 'enminded' into disciplinary genres: Crossing biographic and situated knowledge. *Learning and Instruction, 10,* 331–59.

Tochon, F.V. (2001a). Education research: new avenues for video pedagogy and feedback in teacher education. *International Journal of Applied Semiotics, 2*(1–2), 9–28.

Tochon, F.V. (2001b). Orientation réflexive et sens communautaire à l'arrivée d'une période troublante [Reflective trend and sense of community in troubled times]. *Revue Carrefours de l'éducation* (Université d'Amiens), *12,* 3–28.

Tochon, F.V. (Ed.). (2002a). *The foreign self: Truth telling as educational inquiry.* Madison, WI: Atwood.

Tochon, F.V. (Ed.). (2002b). Semiotic consciousness [Special issue]. *International Journal of Applied Semiotics, 3*(2).

Trungpa, C. (1973). *Cutting through spiritual materialism.* Denver: University of Colorado Press.

Turnbull, D. (1993). *Maps are territories: Science is an atlas.* Chicago: University of Chicago Press.

Van Dijk, T.A. (1973). Grammaires textuelles et structures narrative. [Text grammars and narrative structures]. In C. Chabrol (Ed.), *Sémiotique narrative et textuelle* [Semiotic of the text and story] (pp. 177–206). Paris: Larousse University Press.

Van Manen, M. (2001). *Moral language and pedagogical experience.* Edmonton: University of Alberta, http://www.ualberta/~vanmanen/moral_language.htm

Viens, J.G. (1991, November). *Mots-clés, hypermédias et enseignement: Aller au-delà de la fonction d'indexation pour une meilleure intégration pédagogique* [Keywords, hypermedia, and teaching: Beyond indexation for a better pedagogical integration]. Paper presented at the third Association Canadienne-Française pour l'Avancement des Sciences. ACFAS Conferencey. Ottawa, ON.

von Humboldt, W. (1936/1974). *Introduction à l'oeuvre sur le kavi et autres essais* [Introduction to work on Kavi and other essays]. Paris: Seuil.

Waddington, T.S.H. (1995, April). *Why mastery matters.* Paper presented at the annual meeting of the American Educational Reseach Association (AERA), San Francisco.

Weinstein, C.E., Goetz, E.T., & Alexander, P.A. (1988). *Learning and study strategies: Issues in assessment, instruction, and evaluation.* New York: Academic Press.

White, H. (1978). *Tropics of discourse: Essays in cultural criticism.* Baltimore: MD: Johns Hopkins University Press.

Whitson, J.A. (1992, April). *Cognition as a semiosic process: Grounding, mediation, and critical reflective transcendence.* Paper presented at the annual meeting of the American Educational Reseach Association (AERA), San Francisco.

Winograd, P., & Hare, V.C. (1988). Direct instruction of reading comprehension strategies: The nature of teacher explanation. In C.E. Weinstein, E.T. Goetz, & P.A. Alexander (Eds.), *Learning and study strategies: Issues in assessment, instruction, and evaluation* (pp. 121–39). New York: Academic Press.

Wittgenstein, L. (1999) *Philosophical investigations* (G. E. M. Anscombe, Trans.). Upper Saddle River, NJ: Prentice Hall. (Original work published 1953)

Wortham, S. (1994). *Acting out participant examples in the classroom.* Philadelphia: John Benjamins.

Zay, D., & Day, C.F. (1998, September). *Conceptualizing reflective practice through researchers/practitioners partnerships: A discussion of dilemmas.* Paper presented at the Colloquium of the European Educational Research Association, Ljutljana, Slovenia.

Zeichner, K.M. (1994). Research on teacher thinking and different views of reflective practice in teaching and teacher education. In I. Calgren, G. Handal, & S. Vaage (Eds.), *Teachers' minds and actions: Research on teachers' thinking and practice* (pp. 9–27). London: Falmer Press.

Zeni, J. (Ed.). (2001). *Ethical issues in practitioner research.* New York: Teachers College Press.

Name Index

Abu'l-Barakat al-Baghdadi, 86
Aguirre, 36
Alexander, 22
Al-Farabi, 85
Anderson, 20, 24
Andress, 74
Apple, 44, 132
Arendt, 49
Aristotle, 83, 92, 131
Avicenna, 85, 135

Bachelard, 109
Balzac, 70
Bangert-Drowns, 17
Banks, 31
Barone, 35, 71
Barthes, 11, 75
Bateson, 123
Benetton, 132
Bereiter, 24
Bertrand, 7, 110
Bibby, 27
Block, 14–16
Bloom, 16–17, 20, 38, 121
Brown, 8
Bruner, 8, 32, 68
Buber, 34

Buchmann, 36
Buckley, 24
Burns, 14, 16, 18, 19
Byrne, 14

Cage, 106
Carr, 22
Carroll, 15, 18
Castaneda, 34
Castells, 94
Castoriadis, 123
Chandler, 32
Chevallard, 27
Chipman, 21
Chliwniak, 36
Clandinin, 31, 34, 46, 49, 50, 63, 64
Cochran-Smith, 30, 39
Connell, 28
Connelly, 31, 34, 46, 49, 63, 64
Cooper, 24
Courtés, 51, 53, 57
Csikszentmihalyi, 111

Dalpé, 115–16, 120
Danesi, 8, 50
Day, 29, 38
Delors, 139

Subject Index